ROUTLEDGE LIBRARY EDITIONS:
SOVIET POLITICS

Volume 13

SOVIET COMMUNISM

SOVIET COMMUNISM

Programme and Rules

STEPHEN WHITE

Routledge
Taylor & Francis Group

LONDON AND NEW YORK

First published in 1989 by Routledge

This edition first published in 2024
by Routledge
4 Park Square, Milton Park, Abingdon, Oxon OX14 4RN

and by Routledge
605 Third Avenue, New York, NY 10158

Routledge is an imprint of the Taylor & Francis Group, an informa business

British Library Cataloguing in Publication Data
A catalogue record for this book is available from the British Library

ISBN: 978-1-032-67165-9 (Set)
ISBN: 978-1-032-67498-8 (Volume 13) (hbk)
ISBN: 978-1-032-67505-3 (Volume 13) (pbk)
ISBN: 978-1-032-67501-5 (Volume 13) (ebk)

DOI: 10.4324/9781032675015

Publisher's Note
The publisher has gone to great lengths to ensure the quality of this reprint but
points out that some imperfections in the original copies may be apparent.

Disclaimer
The publisher has made every effort to trace copyright holders and would
welcome correspondence from those they have been unable to trace.

Soviet Communism: Programme and Rules

Stephen White

Department of Politics
University of Glasgow

Programme and Rules translated
by the Novosti Press Agency

R

Routledge
London and New York

First published 1989
by Routledge
11 New Fetter Lane, London EC4P 4EE
29 West 35th Street, New York, NY 10001

© 1989 Stephen White

Filmset by Mayhew Typesetting, Bristol, England
Printed in Great Britain by
Billing & Sons Ltd, Worcester

British Library Cataloguing in Publication Data

Kommunisticheskaia partia Sovetskogo Soiuza
    Soviet communism: programme and rules of the
    Soviet Communist Party
    1. Soviet Union. Political parties: kommunisticheskaia
    partiia Sovetskogo Soiuza. Policies
    I. Title   II. White, Stephen, *1945–*
    324.247'075
    ISBN 0-415-03479-5

Library of Congress Cataloging in Publication Data

Soviet communism : programme and rules / Stephen White :
    programme and rules translated by the Novosti Press Agency.
        p. cm.
    ISBN 0–415–03479–5
    1. Communism — Soviet Union. 2. Kommunisticheskaia partiia
Sovetskogo Soiuza. I. White Stephen, 1945–
HX313.5.S69 1989   89–3501
324.247'075 — dc19   CIP

Contents

Preface

The Communist Party of the Soviet Union is the ruling party of the world's largest country, and the Programme and Rules are the documents upon which its activities are based. In 1986, at the 27th Party Congress, new versions were adopted of both the Programme and the Rules, which represented a considerable departure from their Khrushchevite predecessors. In the summer of 1988, at the 19th Party Conference, further changes were agreed in the basis upon which the party should conduct itself in response to the call for 'democratisation' of the Soviet political system launched at the beginning of 1987. This volume contains the full text of both the Party Programme and the Party Rules in the authoritative translations issued by the Soviet authorities themselves. In addition, a detailed introduction sets the Programme and Rules in context, considering the manner in which they have evolved since earlier years and the significance of the changes that have now occurred, and giving particular attention to the debates that have taken place over the past two or three years about the changes that should be made in the Programme and Rules and, by extension, in the role of the Communist Party itself in Soviet society.

In preparing this edition I am indebted, first of all, to Novosti Press Agency for permitting me to reproduce the official translations of the Programme and Rules that were issued under their auspices. I am also grateful to the Economic and Social Research Council who have supported my work on Soviet politics in the Gorbachev period and who have enabled me to make a number of study visits to the USSR to consult material not readily available in the UK. This volume is intended to be of value to students of Soviet and comparative politics who require access to the Party Programme and Rules in a convenient form; but it will also, I hope, be of interest to an audience more professionally concerned with the process of political reform that is currently taking place in the USSR.

Stephen White

Introduction

Introduction

Political leaders in the communist world, unlike their liberal-democratic counterparts, do not necessarily claim that the policies they promote are popular or that they have been made by representatives freely chosen to speak in the people's name. Their central claim is rather that the policies they promote are derived from Marxism-Leninism, which is a 'science' of human affairs of universal and eternal validity. Policies informed by Marxism-Leninism are therefore 'correct' and in accordance with the real long-term interests of working people, whatever working people, influenced by 'subjective factors' such as nationalism or material self-interest, might themselves be inclined to think. To some extent the constitutions of communist nations serve as a means of identifying long-term interests of this kind: the current Soviet Constitution, for instance, describes the supreme goal of the Soviet state as the 'building of a classless communist society in which there will be public, communist self-government'.[1] To a much greater extent, however, the long-term objectives of communist leaders are apparent in the programmes to which the ruling parties, as leading and guiding forces in their societies, formally commit themselves. There have so far been three such Party Programmes in the USSR, the main aims of which have been respectively the overthrow of Tsardom, the establishment of socialism, and the transition — still to be accomplished — to a fully communist society.

The Party Programmes of 1903 and 1919

The first Party Programme was adopted in 1903 by the Second Congress of the Russian Social-Democratic Labour Party (RSDLP), from which the CPSU of modern times takes its origin. The party had been founded by a group of Russian, Ukrainian and Jewish socialists at an illegal and far from representative gathering in Minsk in 1898.

The Second Congress of the RSDLP met in Brussels and then reconvened in London in July and August 1903; it was the congress at which the party split into its Menshevik (minority) and Bolshevik (majority) factions, and the first in which the later Soviet leader, V.I. Lenin, was able personally to participate (he spoke more than 120 times[2]). The First Congress had issued no more than a manifesto emphasising that the task of social liberation in Russia was one that must be performed by the working class and had otherwise few practical consequences.[3] The Second Congress in 1903 adopted a rather more elaborate Programme embodying, as was conventional among socialist parties at the time, both 'minimum' and 'maximum' objectives. The 'minimum' part of the Programme, which set out a number of social and political reforms relating to the first or 'bourgeois' stage of the revolution, aroused little controversy; there was much more discussion about the second or 'maximum' part, which related to the ultimate objectives of the proletarian revolution.[4]

The Programme, as adopted, began by identifying the Russian Social Democrats with the 'world-wide army of the proletariat'. Like socialists in other countries, Russian Social Democrats were confronted by an exploitative, capitalist social order, which developed national wealth but at the same time became subject to increasingly grave contradictions. These could only be resolved by a social revolution carried out by the working class, which would 'abolish the class division of society and thereby liberate all oppressed humanity'. A necessary condition for this social revolution was a dictatorship of the proletariat, to overcome the resistance of the exploiters, and an independent political party of the working class. This long-term goal was shared by all socialist parties; shorter-term goals were determined by specific local conditions. In Russia, where capitalism (as Lenin had argued) had become the 'dominant method of production', the immediate aim of the party must be the overthrow of the autocracy and its replacement by a democratic republic. A democratic republic of this kind would in turn carry out a series of social and political reforms in the interests of all working people.

There would, for instance, be a directly elected and sovereign legislative assembly based upon universal adult suffrage. There would be extensive local self-government, unrestricted freedom of conscience, speech, the press and assembly, complete social equality and self-determination for all nationalities. Church and state were to be separated, and a people's militia was to replace the regular army. There was to be free and compulsory education for all children up to the age of sixteen, and all indirect taxes were to be replaced by a graduated income and inheritance tax. A further section covered improvements in working conditions: an eight-hour day with guaranteed time off, a ban on overtime and virtually all night work, and a ban on the employment of minors or of women in occupations that were harmful to their health. The final section concerned the countryside, where unjust payments and restrictions were to be cancelled and excessively high rents abolished in order to eliminate the remnants of serfdom and to 'further the free development of the class struggle'. (These last provisions, however modest, represented the first incorporation of peasant demands into the programme of a European socialist party.[5])

This first Party Programme remained in effect until March 1919, although suggestions were made in 1914 and again in August 1917 that a new version might be needed.[6] As party resolutions throughout this period made clear, the central objective of Russian Social Democrats remained the 'overthrow of Tsardom and the conquest of political power by the proletariat which, with the support of revolutionary sections of the peasantry', would 'complete the bourgeois-democratic revolution by convening a nationwide constituent assembly and setting up a democratic republic'.[7] Some aspects of the Programme were, however, modified or amplified to accord with changing circumstances. The agrarian part of the Programme, for instance, was expanded following the 1905 revolution, in which the peasantry had been unexpectedly active: the party approved the seizure of noble, state, monastic and monarchical land at its Third Congress in 1905,[8] and approved a more far-reaching transfer of land to the control of elected local bodies at its Congress in 1906.[9] The revival of national self-consciousness just before the First World War led both Bolsheviks and Mensheviks to reconsider this part of the Programme, the Bolsheviks interpreting self-determination to include the right of any national group to leave the Russian Empire and form an independent state. The expediency of such a move would, however, be judged from the point of view of the proletarian class struggle, which meant in practice that it would not be conceded under socialist conditions.[10]

It was, in fact, under Soviet and socialist conditions that the party met at its Eighth Congress in 1919 to consider the adoption of a new Party Programme, one that would set out the very different tasks of a party that had now conquered power. The victory of the October Revolution represented the achievement of the longer-term objectives of the 1903 Party Programme and immediately made it redundant. Until a new programme could be adopted the Central Committee advised party bodies to be guided by public decrees, and operated itself according to what Nikolai Bukharin later described as an 'unwritten Programme'.[11] In January 1918 a three-man commission, consisting of Lenin, Bukharin and Grigorii Sokolnikov, was set up to devise a new programme, but such were the circumstances of the time that the commission was unable to hold a single meeting, still less to agree upon a suitable text.[12] The Seventh Party Congress, which met in March 1918, elected a new commission which was given some general directives and instructed to prepare a draft as quickly as possible.[13] The commission completed its work in early 1919 and a draft was published in *Pravda* on 25, 26 and 27 February, three weeks before the Eighth Congress was due to meet. About 200,000 party members took at least a nominal part in the discussion of the programme, which was, *Pravda* noted, the 'world's first communist programme of proletarian dictatorship' and therefore deserving of the closest scrutiny.[14]

The second Party Programme, adopted at the Eighth Party Congress in March 1919, took the October Revolution as its starting-point, and saw it as the beginning of an 'era of world-wide proletarian communist revolution'.[15] The Revolution of 1917 had been the 'inevitable result' of the development of capitalism, which still survived in most advanced countries, and which had been correctly analysed by the old Party Programme of 1903. (Bukharin, who opened discussion at the Congress, thought the earlier introduction should be dropped in favour of an analysis of imperialism, which was the modern form of capitalism, but found himself in a small minority.[16]) Not only, the Programme went on, did capitalism contain the inherent contradictions of which the 1903 Programme had spoken: new forms had developed on the basis of increasing concentration and centralisation, involving the formation of great syndicates, a greater role for finance capital and a competitive struggle for control over markets and resources in other countries. This struggle had led to the 'first great imperialist war' of 1914–18, which had been succeeded by a state of civil war within and between nations. Only a socialist revolution led by the working class could lead mankind out of this situation and to a higher kind of economic order, and its final victory was once again 'inevitable'.

The Programme went on to define the specific aims of the dictatorship of the proletariat in Soviet Russia itself. In politics, mass organisations of the working class (such as the elected Soviets) had been turned into the permanent basis of the state apparatus at all levels. This 'higher type of democratism' would be developed further by means of educational and other measures. The Soviet state already provided the means by which workers and peasants could enjoy the democratic rights that were effectively denied to them under capitalism; in the future, every effort would be made to encourage the fullest possible exercise of those rights. Women had been made formally equal to men within marriage and the family; here, unfortunately, there was still educational work to be done in order to eliminate the 'last traces of former inequality and prejudices, especially among the backward sections of the proletariat and peasantry'. Women would be increasingly freed of domestic duties through the provision of house communes, public canteens, central laundries and nurseries. (These points directly reflected the views of the revolutionary feminist, Alexandra Kollontai, who was a member of the working group that prepared the final version.[17]) Organs of government were to be as close as possible to the people, based upon productive units rather than territorial districts, and drawing the armed forces into their work under the leadership of the urban industrial proletariat.

The Programme dealt next with the national question, where it urged closer relations between the various Soviet nationalities while recognising the right of subject nations to independent statehood (Bukharin argued unavailingly that only the working class should be able to exercise this right, and there were many other objections[18]). In military matters the Programme outlined the means by which a 'class army' would be turned into an 'all-people's socialist militia'. In the legal sphere, more workers were to become involved in assessment and the court system itself was to be simplified; judges were to carry out the 'will of the proletariat' as expressed through its decrees, in their absence relying on their 'socialist conscience'. Schools were to be turned from an agency of the class rule of the bourgeoisie into an 'instrument for the communist regeneration of society', involving free and compulsory education for all to the age of seventeen and a higher education that was accessible to all who wished to study, particularly workers. Workers should also be helped to 'liberate their minds from religious prejudices', while not offending the susceptibilities of genuine believers. In economics, the expropriation of the bourgeoisie was to be completed and first priority given to an increase in the output of basic necessities; this was to be achieved by the 'consolidation of all economic activity in the country according to a general state plan' and by the use of the trade unions to secure genuinely popular control over the productive process.

Other economic objectives included the organisation of large-scale socialist agriculture together with improved performance on the part of individual peasant farmers, with a view not just to raising output but to strengthening relations between town and country and between worker and peasant. A 'resolute struggle' would be waged against the kulak or 'rural bourgeoisie', while less prosperous peasants would be encouraged to side with the poor peasantry who themselves were to organise a network of party cells and other bodies. Private trade was to be replaced gradually by the 'systematic distribution of products on an organised national scale'. The banking system had been turned into an 'instrument of workers' power' and would be gradually abolished altogether as money was eliminated. All capitalist landlords' houses had been expropriated and handed over to city Soviets; further efforts would concentrate upon the rebuilding of old, and construction of new, housing and 'rational resettlement of the working masses'. The progressive labour legislation that had already been introduced was to be strengthened further, leading towards a six-hour day with two further hours spent on economic study, military training and state administration. In public health, finally, the Programme committed the party to a series of 'large-scale sanitary measures in the interest of workers' including legislation and the placing of communal meals on a 'scientific-hygienic basis'.

Khrushchev and the 1961 Party Programme

The 1919 Party Programme was a very influential document, at least in the short term. The communist parties or Soviet republics that were founded in other countries during the same period made considerable use of its formulations; the Hungarian Communist Party, which met in June 1919 during the short-lived Soviet republic in that country, put forward the Soviet Party Programme as the basis of its own, and so too did the Socialist Workers' (in effect Communist) Party of Finland, which was formed in 1920.[19] Bukharin, whose jointly authored *ABC of Communism* was based on the new Programme, called it a 'programme of the international proletariat'.[20] In Soviet Russia itself Lenin had called at the Eighth Congress for the Party Programme to be supplemented by a 'second programme', one concerned with economic reconstruction, and this became GOELRO, the plan for the electrification of the whole country over a period of from ten to fifteen years, which was adopted in 1920. There followed, from the late 1920s onwards, a process of rapid and often coercive social transformation involving the development of heavy industry, the collectivisation of agriculture and a 'cultural revolution' among the population at large, which led to the achievement of what Soviet leaders at the time defined as a fully socialist society by the late 1930s. The 1919 Party Programme, intended to provide guidelines for the establishment of such a society, now found itself overtaken by events.

The first call for revision of the Programme was made as early as

1930 when V.M. Molotov, reporting to the 16th Party Congress, suggested that the party's own Programme should be reformulated along the lines of the Programme of the Communist International, which had been adopted at that organisation's Sixth World Congress two years earlier.[21] The 18th Party Congress in 1939 agreed that the Programme had 'lagged behind our achievements' and elected a commission, headed by Stalin, to prepare a new version of the Party Programme for the following congress. The commission, however, held no publicly recorded meetings and with the outbreak of war the task of preparing a new programme had to be postponed still further.[22] In 1952 at the 19th Party Congress a new committee, headed again by Stalin, was appointed to take charge of the preparation of a new Party Programme and to present it to the party congress immediately following, but once again it failed to do so.[23] The 20th Party Congress in 1956 was told by Khrushchev, Stalin's successor, that no new draft had as yet been prepared; it would, however, be presented to the following congress for its approval, and the Congress resolved that it should be published in time for an extensive public discussion beforehand.[24] The next party congress, in 1959, was an 'extraordinary' one, and it was not until June 1961, shortly before the next regular party congress, that a draft of the new programme was submitted to the Central Committee for its approval.[25]

The new programme was once again published in draft in the national press and became the subject of a wide-ranging, if Soviet-style 'debate'. The figures, as usual, were impressive. Over nine million members, Khrushchev reported, or the 'entire party', had taken part in the discussion at meetings and conferences. Apart from this, over 500,000 meetings were held at which about 73 million ordinary citizens participated, of whom well over 4.6 million took the floor; and 300,000 letters and other proposals had been sent in to party offices and to the newspapers, radio and television.[26] Although the draft had been 'unanimously approved', Khrushchev indicated that some changes had been made in the draft as a result of these discussions. Greater emphasis, for instance, had been placed upon technical progress and the effectiveness of capital investment, conservation of the environment, housing, the expansion of pre-school institutions and a shorter working week for women. Many other shortcomings had been identified which were properly the concern of local party and state bodies.[27] The new third Party Programme, modified as Khrushchev had indicated, was duly endorsed by the Congress on 31 October 1961; Khrushchev himself hailed it as a 'Communist Manifesto of the modern era'.[28]

The Programme consisted of two parts, the first dealing with the transition from capitalism to communism on a global scale, the second with the construction of a fully communist society in the USSR itself.[29] The first part began by recapitulating the analysis of capitalism and imperialism that had been given in earlier Programmes, declaring that system 'ripe for the social revolution of the proletariat'. The world capitalist system had already been breached in Russia, where the October Revolution had established a new kind of state conducting a new kind of relations with other states and peoples. Socialism in the USSR had abolished the exploitation of man by man, encouraging creative work, democracy, social security and scientific advance. A world socialist system had come into being in Europe and Asia, consisting of sovereign peoples united by 'close bonds of international socialist solidarity' (there was no direct reference to the Cuban revolution, nor to the dispute with the Chinese[30]). While the world socialist system was 'advancing steadily towards decisive victory in its economic struggle with capitalism', capitalism itself was seized by a 'general crisis' and had 'for ever' lost its control over the destinies of most of the world's peoples. It was confronted by a world-wide revolutionary movement, supported by the USSR, which would so far as possible seek to accomplish its objectives by peaceful means. This was particularly the case where nuclear weapons were concerned.

The second, slightly longer part of the Programme dealt with the 'tasks of the Communist Party of the Soviet Union in building a communist society'. A society of this kind was a 'classless social system with one form of public ownership of the means of production and full social equality'; its achievement had become an 'immediate practical task for the Soviet people'. During the first stage, from 1961 up to 1970, the material and technical basis of communism would be created and the strongest and richest capitalist country, the USA, would be overtaken in total production. By the end of the following decade (1971–80), a state of abundance would be created and a communist society 'in the main' would be constructed, to be 'fully completed' over the following period. These ambitious overall objectives required the introduction of a high level of technology into the economy, the development of a 'flourishing, versatile and highly productive agriculture', a 'continuous improvement in economic management and planning', and the provision of living standards for working people which were higher than those in any capitalist country. Income differentials would diminish, the demand for high-quality consumer goods would be 'amply satisfied', the housing shortage would be brought to an end, a six-hour working day would be introduced, and more and more services such as public catering would be provided free of charge.

10

The advance towards a fully communist society equally required the further development of Soviet democracy. The state was no longer one of the dictatorship of the proletariat but one 'of the entire people', expressing the interests and will of all sections of the community. The role of the elected Soviets would expand, and working people would be involved to a much greater extent in their work. The most important laws would be submitted to a nationwide referendum; judicial punishment would gradually be replaced by 'measures of public influence and education'; and the role of voluntary bodies such as the trade unions would become much greater. Socialist statehood would gradually develop into 'communist self-government' based upon the active participation of all members of the society in the management of public affairs. Relations between the different Soviet nationalities would become closer until eventually complete unity was achieved; and a 'new man' would be brought into being through ideological work and the influence of communist forms of social organisation. A 'moral code of the builder of communism' was set out in this connection, embracing devotion to the communist cause, conscientious labour for the good of society, a high sense of civic responsibility, collectivism, honesty and material disinterestedness. The Programme concluded with the ringing declaration: 'The party solemnly proclaims: The present generation of Soviet people shall live under communism!'

For all its grandiloquence, the 1961 Programme did break new ground in ideological terms as compared with its two predecessors. This was particularly the case in international relations, where the Programme committed the party more firmly than ever before to what was called the 'Leninist principle of the peaceful coexistence of states with different social systems'. Greater emphasis than before was placed upon the peaceful nature of the transition to socialism in capitalist countries: communists, it was explained, would 'prefer to achieve the transfer of power from the bourgeoisie to the proletariat by peaceful means, without civil war'. A more positive attitude was taken towards the colonial and newly independent countries, which were no longer seen as appendages of the major capitalist powers but as a 'progressive, revolutionary and anti-imperialist force' of their own with a common interest in peace and socialism. Pacifism and disarmament were given official approval in a Party Programme for the first time. There was novelty also in the Programme's claim that the CPSU had become a party of the whole Soviet people, not just of the proletariat, and in the attempt to place an increasing range of public functions, from sport to public order, in the hands of groups of ordinary citizens. The whole process reflected Khrushchev's own optimistic belief that the USSR had already entered a new period of development, that of the 'full-scale construction of communist society'.[31]

Gorbachev and the 1986 Party Programme

Almost immediately after Khrushchev's fall from power in 1964 Soviet sources began to place less emphasis upon the claim that the USSR was engaged in the full-scale construction of communism and that it would be accomplished within a specific period of time. The language and predictions of the 1961 Programme were not entirely abandoned: as late as November 1967, in his speech on the fiftieth anniversary of the October Revolution, Leonid Brezhnev (who had succeeded Khrushchev as party leader) used the phrase 'full-scale construction of communism' and promised that the third Party Programme — 'a programme of construction of the foundations of communist society' — would be fulfilled.[32] In the same speech, however, Brezhnev made conspicuous use of the phrase 'developed socialist society', a term he had first used in 1965,[33] and this became the official description of the stage of socialist development that the USSR had attained at the 24th Party Congress in 1971. This, it was made clear, was a new and quite specific stage of Soviet development, with its own laws and dynamics, whose further evolution into full communism would be a matter for some unspecified point in the fairly distant future.[34]

The Party Programme of 1961 was clearly difficult to reconcile with these much less optimistic perspectives, and the 26th Party Congress in 1981 duly approved Brezhnev's proposal that a revised version should be prepared. The essentials of the existing Party Programme, Brezhnev argued, were still valid, but twenty years had elapsed since its adoption and there were many developments it failed to record, notably that Soviet society was progressing towards communism through the stage of 'developed socialism'. This was a necessary and 'historically extended' period in the formation of a communist society, which should find its place in the Party Programme. The Programme should also reflect the changes that were occurring in the Soviet economy, and it should seek to establish only basic principles, not to predict detailed changes. There were international developments, equally, that should be included in the Programme, including the closer integration of the socialist countries, the liquidation of colonialism and the emergence of newly independent states of socialist orientation. The conceptualisation of capitalism itself had to be re-thought in the light of the greater role of the military-industrial complex and of transnational corporations.[35] The Central Committee, it was agreed, should amend the

Programme in the light of these developments and submit a new text to the following congress.[36]

Brezhnev died the following year and his successor, Yuri Andropov, duly became chairman of the committee responsible for preparing a new draft of the Programme. Andropov set out his general approach to such matters in a speech in the spring of 1983 in which he emphasised that the Soviet Union was 'only at the beginning' of the long historical stage of developed socialism; there must be no exaggeration of the country's closeness to communism, and no attempt to minimise the contradictions and difficulties that still remained.[37] Discussing the Party Programme more directly, Andropov told the Central Committee in June 1983 that many of its directives had in fact been realised: links between citizens and deputies, for instance, had become closer, and national discussion of major legislative items had become a well-established practice. Some of the assumptions in the Programme, however, had not withstood the test of time, and there were elements of 'detachment from reality, undue anticipation and unnecessary detail'. The new version of the Programme, which was under preparation, would require a 'realistic analysis of the existing situation' and should give 'clear guidelines for the future'.[38]

These emphases were repeated by Andropov's successor, Konstantin Chernenko, who was General Secretary for just over a year from 1984 to 1985. Addressing the commission set up by the Central Committee to prepare the revised Programme in April 1984, Chernenko emphasised the need to remove the 'oversimplified impression of the means and dates by which a transition to the higher stage of communism' would take place. The new draft should provide a 'realistic' and 'thoroughly considered' evaluation of developed socialism, which would, as already announced, be an 'historically protracted period'. Although there had been major achievements, it was more important to focus upon the 'complicated problems' that Soviet society still confronted than to dwell upon what Lenin had called the 'relatively distant, beautiful and rosy future'. Although capitalism, for instance, would eventually be overtaken by socialism, it had substantial and still unexhausted reserves of strength, and future international developments could not be predicted with any certainty. The Programme should concentrate upon the foreseeable future and immediately attainable tasks, and should at all costs avoid 'unfounded promises and prognoses'; it should also be relatively brief and avoid unnecessary detail.[39]

Chernenko was succeeded in March 1985 by Mikhail Gorbachev, not only as General Secretary but also (it emerged) as chairman of the commission preparing the new version of the Party Programme.[40]

Events now moved quickly. On 26 September 1985 the Politburo approved draft versions of the new Programme and of a revised set of Party Rules; on 14 October the programme commission met again and approved a revised draft; the following day this revised draft was approved by the Central Committee; and finally on 26 October, well in advance of the forthcoming congress, the text of the new Programme was published in the central press for discussion in both party and non-party circles.[41] The 26th Party Congress had not specifically called for revisions in the Party Rules, which have greater operational significance, but in August 1984 a Politburo meeting accepted Chernenko's recommendation that a commission be established to consider what changes might be required. The Central Committee approved these changes on 15 October 1985 and then on 2 November a revised statute was published in the central press, also for general party and non-party discussion.[42]

The Discussion of the Party Programme and Rules

The draft Programme had been thoroughly discussed at all levels of the party, Gorbachev told the 27th Congress when it met in February 1986. In addition, some six million letters had come in from ordinary citizens suggesting changes of various kinds. Some, Gorbachev reported, had argued that the notion of developed socialism should disappear altogether from the Programme; others believed it should be dealt with at greater length. The final version, in the event, referred briefly to developed socialism but placed its main emphasis upon the acceleration of socio-economic development, a more distinctively Gorbachevian theme. Other points that had been considered by the commission included unearned income and the misuse of public property, moral and cultural questions and the further democratisation of public life, particularly at the level of the workplace. These and other proposals, Gorbachev reported, had been wholly or partly incorporated into the draft that was presented to the Congress for its approval.[43]

The public discussion was certainly an extensive one. *Pravda*, for instance, received some 25,000 letters directly connected with the Programme, Rules and other Congress documents; the daily *Sovetskaya Rossiya* received even more – some 35,000 by late January 1986, accounting for about half of all the letters the paper had received over the same period.[44] The public discussion of the draft Programme dealt with a wide range of issues. Writers in the party history journal, for instance, suggested that more attention be given to atheistic education and to 'anti-social elements' in Soviet life.[45] It was also suggested that there should be more precision about the stages by which the 'unity' cf the various Soviet nationalities would lead to their eventual 'fusion', a term the original draft had studiously avoided (so, too, did the final version).[46] Writers in the main philosophical journal urged the need for further efforts to achieve social justice, particularly by eliminating unearned incomes and increasing direct taxation ('socialism and the millionaire', it was argued, should be 'mutually irreconcilable phenomena').[47] Many of the journal's correspondents argued for a strengthening of legal controls; others were more concerned about the danger of nuclear war and the threat of ecological catastrophe.[48]

More extended discussion of the draft Programme took place in academic institutions and associations. Legal specialists from the Institute of State and Law of the USSR Academy of Sciences, for instance, suggested that more emphasis be given to the development of a 'legal culture' among the population at large and argued for a greater role for law in the regulation of the economy, perhaps through the adoption of a special Economic Code.[49] G.I. Tunkin, the Soviet Union's leading specialist on international law, added that the section on cooperation with socialist countries should refer not simply to proletarian internationalism but also to respect for state sovereignty and mutual non-interference in internal affairs, if only to counter Western criticisms (in the event this section remained unchanged).[50] A further discussion was organised by the Soviet Association of Political Sciences, which emphasised the contribution that academics had already made to the draft and the contribution they had still to make by spelling out the practical implications of some of the Programme's more general proposals (for instance, that elected Soviets should play a greater part in the conduct of public affairs).[51]

Not surprisingly, perhaps, in view of their greater practical significance, the pre-Congress period saw a still more searching discussion of the draft Party Rules. Altogether, Gorbachev reported to the Congress, about two million citizens had expressed their views on the changes that had been proposed.[52] The changes that they suggested were rather more controversial than those that had been suggested in relation to the Party Programme. Should there, for instance, be a category of 'honorary party members', asked a party official from Yakutia? It was after all 'not a secret' that because of their advanced age and poor health many members were unable to take an active part in the work of their party organisation as the Rules presently required.[53] Another writer, an economics professor from Moscow, thought the candidate stage should last for two years rather than one, and that applicants should be sponsored by five existing members with at least ten years' standing rather than by three members with at least five years' standing in each case.[54] It was also suggested that candidates be required to take a formal examination in political knowledge before admission, and that alcoholism serve as grounds for expulsion.[55]

Still more sensitive issues were raised in the discussion that took place about the party's own internal organisation. It was suggested, for instance, that compulsory turnover rules should be reintroduced, with elected party bodies renewing their membership by at least a third at each successive election and with individual members unable to serve for more than two terms without special permission from a higher instance.[56] It was argued similarly that district and regional party secretaries should not be eligible for re-election more than three times in a row, nor primary party organisation secretaries more than four times.[57] It was proposed that several candidates be nominated for the post of local party secretary, with the result being decided by a secret ballot; it was pointed out that usually the same number of candidates was proposed as seats available and that the act of voting was wholly formal.[58] A maximum age limit was suggested for the holders of all elected party posts.[59] Other suggested changes included the proposal that there be annual conferences during the intervals between party congresses, as had been the case in Lenin's time; that party members dismissed from their posts be regarded as ineligible for other leading positions; and that not simply those who had been found guilty of criminal offences but also those who had actively or passively assisted them be subject to appropriate measures of party discipline.[60]

The changes that were made to the draft Programme and Rules, taken as a whole, were fairly minor. There were, however, some substantive alterations to both documents. The Programme in its final form, for instance, dropped the reference that had been made in the draft to what Lenin had called 'integral socialism' (this may have been intended to replace the Brezhnevite concept of developed socialism, which in the event was allowed to remain). Additions included a reference to the need for 'necessary correctives' in the electoral system (but in what respects remained unclear), and a new passage on the need to improve the finance and credit system. In the section dealing with social policy, reference was made to the need for children to be responsible for the 'tranquil old age' of their parents, and for attention to be given to the 'socially meaningful interests' as well as needs of young people. In the section dealing with the political system a new paragraph was added on work collectives and their role in economic cultural and political life, including the possibility of an eventual transition to the election of foremen and junior management personnel. A new paragraph was added to the section on ideological and educational work dealing with legal education, and the paragraph on atheistic education was considerably expanded. Finally, in the section on foreign policy, the final version of the Programme added a commitment to general and complete disarmament by the end of the century (not simply disarmament as such), in line with Gorbachev's declaration to this effect of 15 January 1986.[61]

The discussion of the Party Rules also led to relatively few substantive changes, although the version approved by the Congress did differ in some respects from the draft which had been published the previous November. The text that was approved, for instance, included a reference to developed socialism in exactly the same terms as in the Party Programme ('The country has entered the stage of developed socialism'). It also included a requirement that party members make a 'maximum contribution to the acceleration of the socio-economic development of the country' (Rule 2). The section on democratic centralism (Rule 19) included a new sub-clause providing for 'collectivism' in the work of party organisations and 'personal responsibility' on the part of individual members. The section providing for party-wide discussion of controversial matters omitted the possibility, contained in the draft, that there might be such a discussion 'if there is no sufficiently solid majority in the Central Committee on major questions of party policy' (Rule 26); and lower party bodies were required to provide 'objective and timely information' to those above them (Rule 28). More extensive changes occurred in the section on the party primary organisation or branch, which in the final version but not in the draft was given the right to concern itself with the 'exemplary behaviour' of members in their social life and to hear reports from members and candidates on their fulfilment of party responsibilities. The text as approved also required party branches to concern themselves with the Soviet patriotism and social activism of members, and with their sobriety (Rule 58).[62]

The 1986 Programme and Rules

The new version of the Party Programme, as approved by the 27th Congress on 1 March 1986, marks a sharp departure from the optimistic document approved under Khrushchev. Perhaps not surprisingly, Gorbachev told the Congress, many correspondents had suggested it be designated a new fourth Party Programme rather than a revision of the third; but the main objective of the 1961 Programme, the attainment of a fully communist society, had not yet been achieved, and the Programme must accordingly remain in force. At the same time, much had changed in Soviet life since the adoption of the 1961 Programme. Not all of its predictions had turned out to be well founded, and its central thesis, the practical implementation of the full-scale construction of communism, had been premature. The 1986 Party Programme was therefore a new edition of its 1961 predecessor, rather than a new Programme as such: it reaffirmed the main goal of the earlier version, the construction of a communist society, but modified the strategy and tactics of attaining that goal in the light of changing circumstances.[63]

The differences between the two documents were certainly striking. The 1961 Programme, for instance, had declared itself to be a 'programme for the building of communist society'; the 1986 version of the Programme describes itself more modestly as a programme for the 'planned all-round perfection of socialism' and for further advance to communism through the country's 'accelerated socio-economic development'. The 1961 Programme had declared that 'socialism alone' could 'put an end to the exploitation of man by man, production anarchy, economic crises, unemployment and the poverty of the people'; the 1986 version claims only that socialism offers 'advantages' and is a 'stage in mankind's progress that is superior to capitalism'. The 1986 version of the Programme contains no separate section on the world socialist system, and does not specifically identify any other countries as socialist; and it speaks of the common commitment of such countries to the 'defence of revolutionary gains' rather than to a 'common great goal – communism' (a term that appears much less frequently than in its predecessor). Rather than arguing, similarly, that the socialist countries were 'advancing steadily towards decisive victory in [their] economic struggle with capitalism', as the 1961 Programme had done, the 1986 version notes simply that capitalism is 'still strong and dangerous' although its historical doom is 'ever more obvious'.

The sections of the Programme dealing with domestic developments open with a definition of communism that is identical to that in the 1961 version: a 'classless social system with one form of public ownership of the means of production and full social equality of all members of society'. Thereafter the 1986 Programme is consistently less specific and more pessimistic in its projections. The dates and stages by which full communism was to be reached in the 1961 Programme disappear entirely (in fact they had been unmentionable in print since just after the fall of Khrushchev). The 1986 version of the Programme notes rather that the party 'does not attempt to foresee in detail the features of complete communism' and warns that 'any attempt to move ahead too fast' is 'doomed to failure and might cause both economic and political losses'. The 1961

Programme promised a 500 per cent increase in industrial production over the following twenty years; the 1986 Programme speaks more modestly of doubling the country's productive potential by the year 2000, an objective also set out in the 12th Five Year Plan which was approved in principle at the same Congress. The 1961 Programme gave detailed consideration to the development of agriculture; the 1986 Programme mentions agriculture almost in passing and gives much more attention to cost accounting, price reform and the reorganisation of management. The collectivist emphases of the 1961 Programme – more and more services such as transport and heating to be provided free of charge, more public catering and collective upbringing of children – disappear entirely in the 1986 version, together with the promise of a one-month paid holiday for all citizens. In 1961, every family was promised a separate and comfortable flat; in 1986 'practically all' families are promised such accommodation by the end of the century.

There are rather more elements of continuity in the sections of both Programmes that refer to state and public life, where the participatory rhetoric of the Khrushchev period is less at odds with the 'democratising' objectives of the Gorbachev leadership. The development of socialist self-government is, however, conceived in the 1986 version more in terms of the fulfilment of party policy than in terms of popular initiative through the Soviets. There is no mention in the 1986 Programme of government bodies losing their political character and becoming organs of public self-government, nor of the withering away of the state, a central goal of classical Marxism. The 1961 Programme, more specifically, called for at least one-third of the membership of all Soviets to be renewed at each election so that more and more working people could learn to govern the state; the 1986 version calls simply for 'systematic renewal' of their membership. Both versions of the Programme call for greater use to be made of the referendum; Gorbachev, in his speech to the Congress, specifically promised legislation on the matter, which suggested that some exercises of this kind might in fact be conducted in future years.[64] The 1986 Programme none the less sounds a much harsher note in its remarks about discipline (careerism, nepotism and so forth are to be 'relentlessly rooted out and severely punished') and also about the elimination of unearned incomes, parasitism and profiteering. Khrushchev's 'Moral Code of the Builder of Communism' disappears entirely, as it did from the Party Rules;[65] so also do the provisions of the 1961 Programme relating to the compulsory turnover of party bodies. The 1986 Programme, by contrast, deals more extensively with foreign policy and with internal party discipline.

The final text of the Party Rules was approved by the Party Congress on the same date, 1 March 1986. The degree of change as compared with the previous version was rather less than reform-minded correspondents or perhaps even Gorbachev himself might have wished. The new Rules as approved by the Congress did incorporate some reorganisation and rephrasing as compared with their predecessor of 1961, which had already been revised in 1966 and 1971.[66] There were references in the new Preamble, for instance, to Gorbachevian themes such as 'broad publicity', 'accelerated socio-economic development' and 'peace'. More significant changes occurred in Rule 2, which defines the duties of party members. Members are now required to work for the 'application of modern achievements in science and technology to the country's economy'; they must 'assert the principle of social justice which is inherent in socialism' and be 'truthful and honest with the party and the people'; and they must struggle not only against ostentation, conceit and complacency but also against 'eyewash', 'bureaucratism' and 'departmentalism'. In Rule 3 members are given the right (hitherto an almost entirely nominal one) to criticise 'any party body' as well as any other party member. Applicants up to the age of twenty-five, rather than twenty-three as previously, must now join the party through the Komsomol, and decisions on membership are normally to be made at open party meetings (Rule 4). The section on party discipline (Rule 9) has become more detailed, with the main responsibility for enforcement being vested in the primary party organisations. Appeals against expulsion must now be heard within two months, rather than one month as previously (Rule 13). A quorum is specified for the first time for party conferences and congresses (Rule 22); and party secretaries at area, city and district level, together with the heads of political directorates in the armed forces, must have at least five rather than three years' party standing (Rules 49 and 68).

A number of other changes were of rather more consequence. The new Rule 12, for instance, specifies that party members must bear a dual responsibility to the state and to the party for violations of the law, ending the immunity under which party members could in practice be prosecuted for criminal offences only after their expulsion from the party.[67] The party apparatus is referred to for the first time in the new Rules, with responsibilities which include verification of the fulfilment of party decisions and 'rendering assistance to lower organisations in their activities' (Rule 23). The principle of collective leadership (Rule 27) is now held to exclude 'volitional, subjectivist decisions', clearly a reference to Khrushchev. The party congress has been empowered to examine and decide upon the most important questions of 'party and state life' (the latter surely a constitutional anomaly) rather than simply questions of 'communist construction' (Rule 33). The Central Auditing Commission has been given more fully specified responsibilities, including the handling of 'letters, submissions and complaints from the working people' (Rule 36). More far-reaching changes affect the primary party organisation (PPO), the 'basis of the party' as the Rules continue to describe it. The PPO bureau is henceforward to be elected for two or three years, rather than one year as previously; it is, however, required to keep party members regularly informed of its activities (Rule 56). The PPO itself has been given an expanded list of responsibilities, including taking an 'active part in implementing the party's personnel policy' (approving the appointment of key officials) as well as monitoring working and living conditions and directing the work of Komsomol, trade union and other social organisations (Rule 58).

The Debate Continues

The conclusion of the 27th Party Congress should, in theory, have ended the discussion of the Party Rules and Programme, as only a party congress, convened every five years, has the right to adopt or amend these documents. Gorbachev had therefore no obvious means of altering the rules of the Soviet political game before the 28th Party Congress, due in 1991. The Party Rules, however, also provide for party conferences, saying very little about them other than that they may be called 'whenever necessary' in order to discuss 'urgent questions of party policy' (Rule 40). No such gathering had taken place since the 18th Party Conference which met in 1941, just before the outbreak of the war with Nazi Germany; indeed for part of the intervening period (between 1952 and 1966) the relevant provision had been dropped altogether from the Party Rules.[68] The decision to convene a 19th Party Conference in the summer of 1988 was therefore a considerable surprise, not just outside the USSR but also within it, and there was a great deal of speculation about the matters with which it was likely to be concerned.[69]

In the early years of Soviet rule party conferences had in fact taken place as often as party congresses and had played a role in party decision-making that was hardly less significant. The 18th Party Conference in 1941, for instance, approved the economic plan for that year and made additions to the membership of the Central Committee;[70] and the 16th Party Conference, in 1929, had approved the first Five Year Plan.[71] Earlier party conferences had played a role of some significance in the defeat of the Left Opposition during the 1920s, especially the 13th Party Conference in 1924 and the 15th in 1926;[72] still earlier conferences had adopted new editions of the Party Rules (in 1919 and 1922)[73] and (in 1921) had approved an extensive reorganisation of the party's administrative structure.[74] No party conferences, however, had been held from 1932 to 1941, and although some of the East European communist parties had held conferences during the 1980s the decision to hold a party conference after so long an interval was certainly unexpected.

The idea of holding a party conference first emerged publicly in Gorbachev's speech to the January 1987 plenary meeting of the Central Committee, at which the strategy of 'democratisation' was officially approved. It might perhaps be appropriate, Gorbachev suggested to the meeting, to convene an all-union party conference the following year, in order to review implementation of the decisions of the recent Party Congress and to discuss the 'further democratisation of the life of the party and of society as a whole'.[75] The plenum made no direct reference to the holding of a party conference in the resolution with which it concluded, but at the following Central Committee meeting, in June 1987, the proposal was formally approved. There had been a time, Gorbachev reminded the plenum, when conferences had regularly been held in the intervals between party congresses; they had considered major issues of party policy, and had sometimes amended the Party Rules and changed the composition of the Central Committee.[76] It was agreed that a 19th Party Conference should be called the following June with a two-point agenda: first, it should consider the implementation of the decisions of the previous Party Congress; and second, it should consider 'measures for the further democratisation of the life of party and society'.[77] Gorbachev expressed his own belief that the conference would help to democratise inner-party life and that it would lead to a 'deepening of *perestroika* as a whole';[78] yet little had been decided other than that there should be a conference. What it would be invited to consider became the subject of an open and intense political struggle that lasted right up to the Conference itself.

One of the central issues in the debate that took place in the Soviet press and in specialist journals was the further reform of the Communist Party itself. The party theoretical journal, *Kommunist*, argued directly in an editorial in January 1988 that there should be a more restricted understanding of the party's leading role, allowing for a kind of 'division of labour' in which the party would stand aside from day-to-day economic management and exercise a much more general coordinating role.[79] So far as the party's own

22

organisation was concerned a whole series of suggestions were made seeking to introduce more democratic norms. Some correspondents, for instance, argued that party officials should be required to spend four days a week working 'with the masses', leaving the fifth day of the week for paperwork. Others suggested that there should be more regular all-party discussions, as in Lenin's time, and that all executive bodies from the Politburo down should be required to present annual reports.[80] There was a suggestion that party congresses should meet every two years and that party conferences should be held every other year, as in the early days of Soviet rule.[81] And there was a good deal of concern about the way in which the party's own revenues were handled, with calls for elected bodies at all levels to present proper income and expenditure accounts.[82]

Perhaps the most widely supported proposals were that there should be a choice of candidates in all elections to party office, and that positions of this kind should be held for a limited period. Under the existing system of recommendations from above, one correspondent noted, party posts were filled not by election but by nomination, and very often for life.[83] Instead of this, it was argued that there should be a 'periodic renewal of elected and non-elected cadres', with maximum periods of tenure.[84] There should, for instance, be a maximum period of continuous membership of the Central Committee and of its apparatus.[85] Other correspondents suggested a normal limit of two and a maximum of three terms in the same elected party position.[86] One writer suggested restoring the compulsory turnover rule that had been introduced by Khrushchev in 1961 but dropped by his successors in 1966.[87] Another writer in the same journal insisted that there must be more candidates nominated than seats available in elections to party committees, with the result being determined by secret ballot; it should also be possible to change the membership of party committees ahead of time if they were working ineffectively.[88] In addition, age limits were suggested for the holders of leading posts, such as sixty-five in the case of Politburo and Secretariat members.[89]

Changes were also urged in recruitment policy. Greater attention should be given to the purely political qualities of new members, argued a letter in the theoretical journal, *Kommunist*, and the obsession with working-class recruitment should be reduced or ended. Party workers were being 'hypnotised' by the word 'worker' and had been sparing no effort to press them into the ranks provided they were at least non-drinkers and fulfilled their work norms. Not surprisingly, many were rather passive members; but party secretaries, given a 'percentage' by their immediate superiors, had no real alternative but to attempt to satisfy it by recruiting as many workers as would sign an application form. It was difficult, given this mechanical approach to recruitment, to involve non-workers, and party branches were increasingly dominated by workers and pensioners, not those who were advancing scientific-technical progress or the other tasks of *perestroika*. In future, argued the writer (the party secretary of a local telephone station), recruits should simply be the best representatives of the people, whether they were advanced workers or advanced engineers.[90] There was a related discussion of the place of pensioners in the party: some argued that they should be excluded altogether, but others held that this would be 'deeply mistaken' ('a Communist doesn't retire') and that the older generation was not a 'ballast' but a pool of tradition and experience.[91] It should, however, be made possible for those who wished to do so to leave the party voluntarily, perhaps through a periodic process of re-registration;[92] and there was some support for the idea that the party's whole existing membership should be reaccredited and if possible reduced.[93]

There was also strong criticism of the operation of the *nomenklatura* appointments system, especially of its 'closed' character, which led to 'unhealthy elitist and patronising attitudes among some leading cadres'. Some who had been appointed to their positions during the period of stagnation had been found unsuitable for their posts but had all but escaped punishment for the crimes they had committed. Bribe takers and thieves who were on the *nomenklatura* had generally got off with a warning or a horizontal move in the hierarchy, or at the very worst had been retired early with a good pension.[94] There was widespread resentment that the politically influential should have more comfortable flats, better foodstuffs, special hospitals and even (a labour veteran from Krasnodar pointed out) special graveyards.[95] In fact there was a strong case, others argued, for separating party membership from the holding of key positions in order to prevent the party becoming a 'meal ticket' or source of privileges for its members; there had been no difficulty about this in earlier years.[96] Other correspondents suggested reviving the 'party maximum' on earnings that had applied in Lenin's time,[97] or setting up a Committee on Party Ethics.[98]

All of this fell some distance short of securing the proper balance of authority within the party that concerned most contributors to the debate. Towards this end some writers proposed the re-establishment of a Central Control Commission of the kind that had existed in the party during the 1920s and early 1930s, when it served, at least in the view of those who advanced this proposal, as a means of combating bureaucratism and the abuse of elected office. The Central Control Commission of this time had been elected separately by the party congress, and it had been independent of the Central Committee in its decisions and actions.[99] Other correspondents also found the Central Control Commission a helpful precedent in the light of current tasks, providing the basis for a mechanism which would allow the Central Committee and the Politburo itself to be placed under the constant supervision of elected and independent representatives of the party as a whole. Analogous arrangements should apply at the local level. 'How many tragic pages would have been missing in the chronicle of Soviet rule', it was asked, 'if 'defence mechanisms' of this kind had been in existence in earlier times?'[100]

There were further proposals for 'democratising' changes in the functioning of the party's leading bodies. It was argued, for instance, that the Central Committee should play a more active role in the party's affairs, with at least some of its members working together with the Politburo and Secretariat in the preparation of resolutions and of the agenda for plenary meetings.[101] Changes were also suggested in the way in which the Central Committee was itself elected, with the vote taking place at an open session of the party congress and the candidates being identified at least by their place of work.[102] Much more, it was agreed, should be known about how the Central Committee operated, and about what was said and by whom at its plenary meetings.[103] Changes were suggested in the manner in which the General Secretary was elected: rather than the decision being left to a small group working in secret, one correspondent suggested the matter be put to a nationwide vote.[104] Others suggested that party congress delegates decide the matter by secret ballot, or that a 'kind of party referendum' be organised for the purpose.[105] The influential commentator, Fedor Burlatsky, suggested a further option: that the General Secretary be first of all elected at a party congress, but that he should then be nominated for the post of state president with a national ballot being held to confirm the choice, all of this with the aim of moving towards a 'presidential' rather than party-based system of government.[106]

The Party Conference and Political Reform

Gorbachev's report to the 19th Party Conference, which met in Moscow from 28 June to 1 July 1988, dealt with both items of the agenda that had been agreed a year earlier: a review of the implementation of party policy to date, and a consideration of measures for the 'further democratisation of the life of party and society'.[107] The key question, he told the delegates, was how to deepen and make irreversible the process of *perestroika* that was taking place in the USSR under the party's guidance; and the main means of achieving that end, in the leadership's view, was 'radical reform' of the political system. This involved a wide range of changes, including an extension of political rights so as to ensure that all matters of public concern were properly debated and evaluated, and a greater degree of authority for the elected Soviets. The national legislature, the USSR Supreme Soviet, should work on a virtually full-time basis, and the new post of President of the USSR Supreme Soviet should be established to oversee the work of government. Both the President and the working Supreme Soviet would be elected by a new national representative body which would meet annually, the Congress of People's Deputies of the USSR.

Reform of the political system inevitably concerned the CPSU as well as state institutions. The party, just like other areas of public life, had been affected by the 'cult of personality' of the Stalin period and then by the stagnation of the Brezhnev years. Democratic centralism had become bureaucratic centralism, and rank-and-file party members had largely lost their ability to influence party policy. Elected party bodies had lost ground to the full-time apparatus, and an atmosphere of comradeship, tolerant of legitimate differences, had been replaced by one in which some gave orders and others simply carried them out. Many leading officials had begun to feel that they were infallible and irreplaceable, which had sometimes led to their political and moral degradation. The party, Gorbachev suggested, must now remodel its activity and resume its proper role of political vanguard. More specifically, Gorbachev recommended a process of reaccreditation of the existing party membership (this had been suggested in the 'Theses' that were published in the name of the Central Committee shortly before the conference began[108]) and the ending of any 'quotas and bureaucratic methods' in the matter of party membership. The prestige of elected party bodies must also be restored, and ways found of involving Central Committee members in policy formation on a continuing basis, including participation in the work of the Politburo.

Party committees at all levels, Gorbachev went on, must work in a more vigorous and democratic way, and should elect their representatives to higher-level assemblies on the basis of discussion of all the candidates followed by a competitive ballot. Lower-level bodies should also have the right to make recommendations on the choice of candidates to higher-level bodies. More candidates should be nominated than seats available in all party elections, right up to Central Committee level. There should be a uniform five-year term for all party committees, and the holding of elected office should be limited to two terms other than in exceptional circumstances

(Gorbachev acknowledged that there had been some differences of opinion on this point and invited further contributions to the discussion). There must be a clearer differentiation between party and state bodies, with the party relinquishing responsibility for day-to-day management of the economy. There should be no direct party instructions to economic administrators, and the party apparatus at all levels should be reduced in size and in the functions it performed. There had also been approval for the proposal in the Central Committee 'Theses' that a single body be formed to be responsible for discipline and also for party finances.

The debate that followed was unusually open by Soviet standards, and unprecedented in many ways. When, for instance, *Pravda* asked, had a rank-and-file delegate ever disagreed before with one of the General Secretary's proposals (in this case, for the reaccreditation of party membership)?[109] There was a minor sensation when a speaker from the Komi republic, asked to identify some of the opponents of *perestroika*, reeled off a list of names including the Soviet President Andrei Gromyko and the editor of *Pravda*.[110] The dismissed Moscow party secretary, Boris Yeltsin, made an emotional and most unusual speech in which he pleaded for his political rehabilitation.[111] Again without precedent, at least since the early post revolutionary years, was the spectacle of divided votes. A small minority, for instance (145 as against 4,841), supported the idea that the General Secretary should be elected by the party congress rather than by the Central Committee, and 53 delegates voted in favour of *Pravda* becoming an organ of the party as a whole and for its editorial board to be elected at the party congress.[112] Gorbachev, in his closing address, quite reasonably claimed that no gathering of the kind had taken place in the USSR for nearly sixty years.[113]

Discussion at the Conference ranged very widely, from the economy and ecology to women's rights, science, the health service, education and foreign trade. The role of the party and how to restore it to its properly Leninist form was, however, the single most widely-shared concern. There was general agreement, for instance, that the party's primary organisations should be given more autonomy, in financial as in other matters, and that the status of its secretary should be strengthened considerably.[114] Local party organisations should more generally have a greater degree of autonomy, including the right to decide on their own structure and rates of pay.[115] These should certainly be greater: how could party workers be found at 200–220 rubles a month, asked a Kemerovo speaker, when local miners could earn from 500 to 800 rubles over the same period?[116] It was also argued that it should be easier for non-workers to enter the party; political qualities should be decisive, and the inactive 'ballast' should be allowed to leave without dishonour.[117] Careerists and opportunists should perhaps be eliminated from the party by a careful purge, suggested another speaker.[118] There was widespread agreement that elective party posts should be held for two terms only, without any exceptions: this, as Georgii Arbatov, director of the USA and Canada Institute, pointed out, would have brought Stalin's career to an end in 1934 (actually 1932), and Brezhnev's to a close in 1974.[119] Even Gorbachev's general secretaryship, it was agreed, should be limited in this way, despite an emotional appeal from the actor, Mikhail Ulyanov, against 'changing horses in midstream'.[120]

A number of further suggestions were made which were intended, like much of the pre-Conference discussion, to open up the party's internal decision-making processes to ordinary members. There was widespread agreement, for instance, that party members should be better informed of the work of party bodies;[121] more particularly, it was suggested that full reports should be published of Central Committee meetings,[122] and that the positions of individual Politburo and Central Committee members on issues of the day should be made known.[123] An upper age limit of sixty-five was suggested for national and republican party leaders as well as for ministers.[124] Another speaker argued that the structure of the Central Committee and the precise duties of each member of the Politburo and Secretariat should be published; the General Secretary and Politburo members should also publish their programmes before they sought re-election, and it would be a good thing if they were at least slightly different.[125] A Central Control Commission, directly elected by the party congress and with substantial representation from workers and peasants, should be re-established.[126] Renewal of party committees at all levels should become possible in the intervals between their election;[127] and forums like the party conference should be convened more often in view of the rapidly-changing circumstances through which the whole society was living.[128]

This was not to suggest that the delegates were in sympathy with the limited, largely moral role for the party that Gorbachev had sketched out in his opening address. On the contrary, the main concern of most speakers was that the leading role of the party should be reaffirmed and strengthened, without necessarily abandoning any of the mechanisms of control that it had so far accumulated. Appointments, for instance, could not be left to look after themselves, in the view of both the Kirgiz and Moldavian party leaders.[129] The party, argued the rector of Moscow University, could not in practice relinquish its responsibility for management of the economy;[130] nor was there a structure of command in local areas to which the party could as yet surrender its role.[131] There were indignant attacks upon those who had, for instance, tried to separate the CPSU from the state and the society or to exclude it from direction of the economy.[132] The party apparatus, in the view of the Lithuanian party leader, should not be reduced in size but rather redistributed from upper to intermediate and lower levels.[133] A reduction in the role of the party could have 'unforeseeable consequences', warned the Volgograd party first secretary.[134] The party must not surrender its vanguard role, other speakers insisted, and must do everything possible to strengthen the unit of its ranks.[135] There was little support for the view put forward by the editor of *Izvestiya* that the party could no longer play the 'universal, unlimited role' of the past, and that by assuming such general responsibilities it also collected the blame if anything went wrong.[136]

Responsibility for reconciling these various views about the party's role was vested in the commissions that were set up to draft the Conference resolutions. About 70 delegates were able to address the conference out of the 300 or so who had wished to do so, but a further 150 delegates were able to express their views at one or other of these commission meetings.[137] The outcome of their deliberations in terms of party reform was reflected in the resolution on 'Democratising Soviet society and reforming the political system', one of the six with which the Conference concluded. This reaffirmed the need for the party to refrain from direct intervention in economic and administrative matters, abandoning 'command-style methods of work' and ensuring a 'profound democratisation' of its own internal affairs. This would involve a greater degree of independence for party branches, and greater participation by Central Committee members in the work of the Politburo; it should also involve more regular reporting by the Politburo to the Central Committee, and publication of the minutes of party committee meetings at all levels. Elections to party committees right up to Central Committee level should take place after extensive discussion of the candidates and be resolved by secret ballot, with party members entitled (but not required) to nominate more candidates than seats available. Membership of committees would be for five years at a time, but with the right of conferences held halfway through this period to re-elect up to 20 per cent of the membership. No party leader, not even the General Secretary, should be able to hold his post for more than two terms: this and other measures were seen as a 'major guarantee against stagnation'.[138] These changes would ultimately be incorporated into the Rules of the CPSU; in the meantime, the Central Committee resolved on 29 July 1988, all party organisations should function upon their basis.[139]

Programme, Rules and Politics in the USSR

Gorbachev, in summoning the Party Conference, had pointed out
that previous gatherings of this kind had changed the Party Rules and
altered the composition of the Central Committee. If this had been
his purpose in reviving the ancient practice of holding party
conferences, then the 19th Party Conference must be regarded as a
'defeat on points' for the General Secretary and the reformist
policies with which he is associated.[140] The Party Rules state
clearly that it is the prerogative of the party congress to adopt or
amend the Rules and Party Programme, and no formal change to
either document was made by the 19th Party Conference. Nor were
any changes made in the composition of the Central Committee. The
Conference, as we have noted, none the less decided that future
conferences should be able to re-elect up to a fifth of the Central
Committee membership, and the changes that were proposed in the
party's manner of operation are to apply with immediate effect, even
if they can be formally incorporated into the Party Rules only at the
28th Party Congress in 1991. The effort that has been devoted to
matters of this kind suggests that, for Gorbachev at least, changes
in the Party Programme and particularly in the Party Rules are a
significant political objective.

Both the Party Programme and the Party Rules have, of course,
been all but entirely ignored over long periods of Soviet rule. The
Party Rules of 1939, for instance, specified that party conferences
should take place 'at least once a year . . . for the discussion of
pressing questions of party policy', yet there was only one gathering
of this kind between that date and 1952, when the provision was
dropped entirely.[141] The party rules of the 1930s, similarly,
provided that a party congress should be held 'at least once every
three years', yet never was this interval observed during the 1930s
and no congress at all was held between 1939 and 1952. Solzhenitsyn, in his *Gulag Archipelago*, quotes two Soviet party members of
the 1930s who were arrested and given ten years each for having the
temerity to point out that a party congress, under the statute, was
long overdue.[142] An instance from a much more recent period has
been quoted by Vladimir Voinovich: a group of workers in
Sverdlovsk who were arrested at the beginning of the 1970s for
having distributed copies of the then current Party Programme with
its promise of the speedy construction of a fully communist
society.[143] It was, of course, more common for the Programme or
Rules to be ignored or suppressed, or for them to convey no more
than the barest hint of the massive power enjoyed by the central
leadership and by the full-time apparatus in particular (the key post

of General Secretary was not so much as mentioned in the versions of the Party Rules that obtained up to 1966).[144]

At the same time reforming party leaders such as Khrushchev and Gorbachev have clearly found it useful to seek to further their reforms by securing the appropriate amendments in the Party Programme and Rules, which have remained throughout the basic documents upon which the party organisation is based. Khrushchev sought to institutionalise his vision of a prosperous, self-governing society evolving rapidly towards full communism by securing the adoption of a Party Programme which proclaimed the same objective and of a set of Party Rules which insisted on limited tenure of leading posts and the regular turnover of party officials at all levels. (His successors dropped these provisions at the earliest possible opportunity, in 1966.) Equally, Gorbachev in the 1980s has given his continued attention to the Party Rules and Programme, securing a much more realistic Programme and eventually, after the Party Conference of 1988, a set of *de facto* Party Rules which reintroduce similar requirements in terms of limited tenure, regular turnover and (this time without a precedent) secret and competitive ballots for party committees. The first such ballot took place in the Kemerovo region in February 1987, even before the Party Conference had approved the new practice; both candidates were approved by a regional party secretary but the outcome was genuinely in doubt as between the director of a state farm and the chairman of the local Soviet until a ballot resolved the matter, 29 votes to 20, in favour of the chairman.[145]

It is, of course, quite possible to see the introduction of measures facilitating the replacement of leading officials as little more than a means by which the new General Secretary can more readily remove his political opponents.[146] This does not necessarily invest changes in the Party Rules with any less significance. It seems unreasonable, however, to take no account at all of the political vision which has at least ostensibly inspired such changes. As Gorbachev explained at the Party Conference in 1988, grave deformations in Soviet political life had taken place since the Revolution, in particular the repression of the Stalin period and the stagnation of the Brezhnev years. This had led to a command-based system of political management, conducted through a top-heavy system of ministries. Public life had become unduly 'governmentalised', with central control extending into every sphere of social life, and working people alienated from the system of government that functioned in their name. In its place Gorbachev proposed a 'new image of socialism', one that was deeply humanistic in character and based upon a variety of forms of property, worker participation, the satisfaction of basic needs,

31

genuine popular self-government and international cooperation in the interests of peace and security.[147] It is this image of a reformed socialism that animates the Gorbachev leadership and that lies behind the changes in the Party Rules and Programme it has now succeeded in effecting.

Nor is Gorbachev the only communist reformer who has sought to achieve his ends at least in part by changes in the Party Rules and Programme. In Czechoslovakia, for instance, the reform movement of 1968 led to the formulation of a set of party rules which, at least in their initial version, allowed minorities within the party, even if defeated, to persist in their views and to call for an issue to be reopened if new evidence appeared to require it. Minority views were to be published in the party press alongside those of the majority, and party members were to be allowed to associate with each other 'temporarily' on a horizontal basis for the purposes of consultation, exchanges of information and even joint campaigns.[148] In Poland the 'renewal' of 1980–1 led to the adoption of a still more remarkable set of statutes which provided that candidates for party office should always exceed the number of vacancies, permitted horizontal links among party members and allowed minorities the right to express dissenting views even though their actions must always accord with those of the majority. Party members were prohibited from holding more than two elected posts at the same time, and a strict separation was introduced between party, state and associational office-holding at the same level. The same provisions are contained in the Rules of the Yugoslav ruling party, the League of Communists.[149]

The evidence suggests, then, that Gorbachev may have some justification for including the Party Programme and Rules within the scope of his reforming objectives. The Party Programme sets out the official ideology in a concise and policy-relevant form, providing broad guidelines for the formulation of more detailed objectives by officials at all levels of the system. The Programme adopted in 1986 gives a very clear sense of the leadership's belief that talk of the communist future is not simply premature but positively harmful in present circumstances, and that much more importance is to be placed upon the achievement of practical tasks in the relatively short term. The Party Rules as they now stand, similarly, reflect Gorbachev's own view that the difficulties presently confronting Soviet society stem from the breakdown of democratic mechanisms during the 1930s, which allowed political leaders at all levels to become remote, self-willed, inactive and sometimes corrupt. The Party Rules of 1986, modified still further by the Conference of 1988, should at least ensure that the party's own procedures are violated less easily in the future than in the recent past. The contribution that political reforms of this kind may make to the larger tasks of *perestroika* is, however, less easy to discern and may well be rather less than the General Secretary appears to have assumed.

Notes

1 *Konstitutsiya (Osnovnoi zakon) Soyuza Sovetskikh Sotsialisticheskikh Respublik* (Moscow: Izdatel'stvo politicheskoi literatury, 1978), p. 5.
2 N.N. Maslov, N.V. Romanovskii and A.A. Chernobaev, *Znamya boryushcheisya partii. Ocherki istorii Programmy KPSS* (Moscow: Izdatel'stvo politicheskoi literatury, 1986), p. 55.
3 *Pervyi s''ezd RSDRP mart 1898 goda. Dokumenty i materialy* (Moscow: Gosudarstvennoe izdatel'stvo politicheskoi literatury, 1958), pp. 79–81. The manifesto is conveniently reprinted in *KPSS v rezolyutsiyakh i resheniyakh s''ezdov, konferentsii i plenumov Ts.K.* [hereafter *KPSS v rez.*], 9th edn, 14 vols (Moscow: Izdatel'stvo politicheskoi literatury, 1983–7), vol. 1, pp. 15–17; an English translation is available in R.H. McNeal (ed.), *Resolutions and Decisions of the CPSU*, 4 vols (Toronto: University of Toronto Press, 1974), vol. 1, pp. 34–6.
4 For the text see *Vtoroi s''ezd RSDRP. Protokoly* (Moscow: Gosudarstvennoe izdatel'stvo politicheskoi literatury, 1959), pp. 418–24. The 1903 Programme is reprinted in *KPSS v rez.*, vol. 1, pp. 59–65, and together with the texts of all other editions of the Programme and Rules in *Programmy i ustavy KPSS* (Moscow: Izdatel'stvo politicheskoi literatury, 1969). An English text is available in McNeal (ed.), *Resolutions*, vol. 1, pp. 39–45; the proceedings of the Congress as a whole are translated in *1903 Second Ordinary Congress of the RSDLP*, trans. Brian Pearce (London: New Park, 1978).
5 Ralph Carter Elwood, in McNeal (ed.), *Resolutions*, vol. 1, p. 38. For further discussion of the 1903 Programme see Leonard Schapiro, *The Communist Party of the Soviet Union*, revised edn (London: Eyre & Spottiswoode, 1970), pp. 44–8, and Maslov *et al.*, *Znamya*, which emphasises the 'decisive contribution' of Lenin (p. 27).
6 Elwood, in McNeal (ed.), *Resolutions*, p. 4.
7 *KPSS v rez.*, vol. 1, pp. 312–14.
8 Ibid., p. 129.
9 Ibid., pp. 194–5.
10 Ibid., pp. 446–7. My discussion of these points is much indebted to Elwood, in McNeal (ed.), *Resolutions*, pp. 3–5.
11 Maslov *et al.*, *Znamya*, p. 95; Bukharin in *Vos'moi s''ezd RKP(b) mart 1919 goda. Protokoly* (Moscow: Gosudarstvennoe izdatel'stvo politicheskoi literatury, 1959), p. 34.
12 Maslov *et al.*, *Znamya*, p. 96.
13 *KPSS v rez.*, vol. 2, pp. 27–8.
14 *Pravda*, 27 February 1918, p. 1; Maslov *et al.*, *Znamya*, pp. 100–1.

15 For the text see *Vos'moi s"ezd*, pp. 390–411. The Programme is also available in *KPSS v rez.*, vol. 2, pp. 71–92, and in *Programmy i ustavy KPSS*. For English versions, see McNeal, (ed.), *Resolutions*, vol. 2, pp. 54–73, and Jan F. Triska (ed.), *Soviet Communism: Programs and Rules* (San Francisco: Chandler, 1962), pp. 130–53.

16 *Vos'moi s"ezd*, p. 45.

17 Maslov *et al.*, *Znamya*, p. 107.

18 *Vos'moi s"ezd*, pp. 46–8, 80, 87.

19 Maslov *et al.*, *Znamya*, pp. 113–14.

20 *Vos'moi s"ezd*, p. 37.

21 *XVI s"ezd Vsesoyuznoi Kommunisticheskoi partii (bol'shevikov). Stenograficheskii otchet* (Moscow-Leningrad: Ogiz, 1931), p. 427.

22 *XVIII s"ezd Vsesoyuznoi Kommunisticheskoi partii (bol'shevikov) 10–21 marta 1939 goda. Stenograficheskii otchet* (Moscow: Ogiz, 1939), pp. 634–5, 687.

23 *Pravda*, 14 October 1952, p. 3, and 9 October 1952, p. 1. Revision of the Programme was to be guided by the fundamental theses of Comrade Stalin's work, 'Economic Problems of Socialism in the USSR' (ibid.)

24 *XX s"ezd Kommunisticheskoi partii Sovetskogo Soyuza 14–25 fevralya 1956 goda. Stenograficheskii otchet*, 2 vols (Moscow: Gosudarstvennoe izdatel'stvo politicheskoi literatury, 1956), vol. 1, pp. 114–15, and vol. 2, p. 499.

25 *KPSS v rez.*, vol. 10, p. 56.

26 *XXII s"ezd Kommunisticheskoi partii Sovetskogo soyuza 17–31 oktyabrya 1961 goda. Stenograficheskii otchet*, 3 vols (Moscow: Gosudarstvennoe izdatel'stvo politicheskoi literatury, 1962), vol. 1, p. 237.

27 Ibid., pp. 238–41. For a more detailed account of the discussion, see Leonard Schapiro (ed.), *The USSR and the Future* (New York: Praeger, 1963), pp. 8–20.

28 *XXII s"ezd*, vol. 1, p. 148.

29 For the text see ibid., vol. 3, pp. 229–335. The Programme is also available in *KPSS v rez.*, vol. 9, pp. 81–185, in *Programmy i ustavy KPSS*, and as a separate publication. English translations are available in McNeal (ed.), *Resolutions*, vol. 4, pp. 167–264, Schapiro (ed.), *The USSR and the Future*, pp. 255–312, and as a separate publication. The version printed in *Current Soviet Policies IV* (New York and London: Columbia University Press, 1962), pp. 1–33, indicates the changes that were made as compared with the draft; so, too, does Triska (ed.), *Soviet Communism*, pp. 23–129.

30 The Cuban revolution was, however, referred to by Khrushchev in his speech: *XXII s"ezd*, vol. 1, p. 229.

31 Alfred B. Evans, 'Developed Socialism and the New Programme of the CPSU', in Stephen White and Alex Pravda (eds.), *Ideology and Soviet Politics* (London: Macmillan, 1988), p. 91; Schapiro, *Communist Party*, pp. 606–7. A fuller discussion of the 1961 Programme is available in Schapiro (ed.), *The USSR and the Future*.

32 Evans, 'Developed Socialism', p. 94. Brezhnev's speech is in his *Leninskim kursom* (Moscow: Izdatel'stvo politicheskoi literatury, 1970),

vol. 2, pp. 75–145.

33 Brezhnev, *Leninskim kursom* (1970), vol. 1, p. 187.

34 Evans, 'Developed Socialism', p. 94.

35 *XXVI s''ezd Kommunisticheskoi partii Sovetskogo Soyuza 23 fevralya – 3 marta 1981 goda. Stenograficheskii otchet*, 3 vols (Moscow: Izdatel'stvo politicheskoi literatury, 1981), vol. 1, pp. 97–8.

36 Ibid., p. 376.

37 Yu.V. Andropov, *Izbrannye rechi i stat'i*, 2nd edn (Moscow: Politizdat, 1983), pp. 245–6.

38 *Pravda*, 16 June 1983, pp. 1–2.

39 Ibid., 26 April 1984, p. 1.

40 Ibid., 30 June 1985, p. 1.

41 Ibid., 27 September 1985, p. 1, 15 October 1985, p. 1, 16 October 1985, pp. 1–2, and 26 October 1985, pp. 1–7.

42 Ibid., 24 August 1984, p. 1, 16 October 1985, p. 1, and (for the draft) 2 November 1985, pp. 1–2.

43 *XXVII s''ezd Kommunisticheskoi partii Sovetskogo Soyuza 25 fevralya – 6 marta 1986 goda. Stenograficheskii otchet*, 3 vols (Moscow: Politizdat, 1986), vol. 1, pp. 116–19.

44 *Voprosy istorii KPSS*, 1986, no. 5, p. 27.

45 Ibid., no. 2, pp. 47, 63.

46 Ibid., pp. 41, 69. The term 'fusion' (*sliyanie*) had not been included in the 1961 Programme, although it had been used in speeches made to the Congress at which it was adopted: see Peter Duncan, 'Ideology and the National Question', in White and Pravda (eds), *Ideology and Soviet Politics*, p. 187.

47 *Voprosy filosofii*, 1986, no. 2, p. 75.

48 Ibid., pp. 77, 77–8.

49 *Sovetskoe gosudarstvo i pravo*, 1986, no. 2, pp. 27, 28.

50 Ibid., p. 50.

51 *Razvivayushchiesya strany v mirovoi politike. Ezhegodnik Sovetskoi assotsiatsii politicheskikh nauk, 1986* (Moscow: Nauka, 1987), pp. 262–5.

52 *Pravda*, 26 February 1986, p. 10.

53 *Kommunist*, 1985, no. 18, p. 61.

54 Ibid., no. 17, p. 79; similarly *Partiinaya zhizn'*, 1986, no. 1, p. 27.

55 *Kommunist*, 1985, no. 17, p. 79.

56 Ibid., pp. 79–80, and no. 18, p. 62.

57 Ibid., no. 17, p. 80.

58 Ibid., p. 82, and no. 18, p. 64.

59 Ibid.

60 Ibid., 1986, no. 1, p. 83, no. 2, p. 85, and no. 1, p. 83.

61 See *Pravda*, 16 January 1986, pp. 1–2. The changes that were made in the final version are indicated in the translation published by the Current Digest of the Soviet Press: see *The Communist Party Program and Party Statutes: Final Versions*, Special Supplement, December 1986.

62 See Stephen White, 'The New Programme and Rules of the CPSU', *Journal of Communist Studies*, vol. 2, no. 2 (June 1986), pp. 182–91,

for an earlier discussion of some of these points.

63 *XXVII s"ezd*, vol. 1, p. 116. For the text of the Programme as adopted see *Pravda*, 7 March 1986, pp. 3–8, and *XXVII s"ezd*, vol. 1, pp. 554–623. A Soviet discussion is available in Maslov *et al.*, *Znamya*, pp. 143–71; the only extended Western commentary is Boris Meissner, *Das Aktionsprogramm Gorbatschows* (Koeln: Verlag Wissenschaft und Politik, 1987).
64 Legislation on 'popular discussion of major questions of state life' was duly adopted by the Supreme Soviet in June 1987: see *Vedomosti Verkhovnogo Soveta SSSR*, 1987, no. 26, item 387.
65 The new Programme did, however, contain a rather shorter passage on 'communist morality': see below, p. 87.
66 For a full discussion of these changes see Graeme Gill, *The Rules of the Communist Party of the Soviet Union* (London: Macmillan, 1988), which contains translations of all the Rules that the party has adopted since 1898; a Soviet commentary is available in O.G. Obichkin, *Kratkii ocherk ustava KPSS*, 2nd edn (Moscow: Politizdat, 1986). For the text of the Rules adopted in 1986, see *Pravda*, 7 March 1986, pp. 8–10, and *XXVII s"ezd*, vol. 1, pp. 624–44.
67 Zhores Medvedev, *Gorbachev* (Oxford: Blackwell, 1986), pp. 222–3.
68 Gill, *Rules*, pp. 47, 63.
69 For a full discussion of the Party Conference see Stephen White, 'Gorbachev, Gorbachevism and the Party Conference', *Journal of Communist Studies*, vol. 4, no. 4 (December 1988).
70 *KPSS v rez.*, vol. 7, p. 192.
71 Ibid., vol. 4, p. 448.
72 Schapiro, *Communist Party*, pp. 306–7, 381.
73 *KPSS v rez.*, vol. 2, pp. 201–9, 573–83.
74 Ibid., p. 419.
75 *Materialy plenuma Tsentral'nogo Komiteta KPSS 27–28 yanvarya 1987 goda* (Moscow: Politizdat, 1987), p. 65.
76 *Materialy plenuma Tsentral'nogo Komiteta KPSS 25–26 iyunya 1987 goda* (Moscow: Politizdat, 1987), pp. 37–8.
77 Ibid., p. 81.
78 Ibid., p. 38.
79 *Kommunist*, 1988, no. 1, p. 6.
80 *Moscow News*, 19 June 1988, p. 2; *Voprosy istorii KPSS*, 1988, no. 6, pp. 44, 46.
81 Ibid., p. 44.
82 *Kommunist*, 1988, no. 3, p. 36.
83 Ibid., p. 37.
84 *Partiinaya zhizn'*, 1988, no. 6, p. 28.
85 *Voprosy istorii KPSS*, 1988, no. 6, p. 44.
86 *Partiinaya zhizn'*, 1988, no. 10, p. 38.
87 Ibid., no. 5, p. 41.
88 Ibid., no. 11, pp. 38–9.
89 *Moscow News*, 10 April 1988, p. 8.
90 *Kommunist*, 1988, no. 4, pp. 85–6.

91 *Partiinaya zhizn'*, 1988, no. 9, p. 47.
92 Ibid., no. 6, pp. 26–7.
93 *Pravda*, 2 May 1988, pp. 1, 3.
94 *Kommunist*, 1988, no. 5, pp. 42, 43–5.
95 *Moscow News*, 24 April 1988, p. 9; similarly *Pravda*, 9 March 1988, p. 2.
96 *Kommunist*, 1988, no. 5, p. 45.
97 *Voprosy istorii KPSS*, 1988, no. 6, p. 45.
98 *Kommunist*, 1988, no. 5, p. 45.
99 Ibid., p. 43.
100 Ibid., no. 6, pp. 30–1.
101 Ibid., no. 9, p. 35.
102 *Moscow News*, 15 May 1988, p. 13.
103 Ibid.; similarly ibid., 24 April 1988, p. 8, and 20 March 1988, p. 8.
104 Ibid., 12 June 1988, p. 8.
105 *Soviet Weekly*, 18 June 1988, p. 10.
106 *Literaturnaya gazeta*, 15 June 1988, p. 2; similarly Melor Sturua in *Moscow News*, 12 June 1988, p. 8.
107 For the speech see *Pravda*, 29 June 1988, pp. 2–7.
108 Text in *Izvestiya*, 27 May 1988, pp. 1–2.
109 *Pravda*, 1 July 1988, p. 1.
110 Ibid., p. 7.
111 Ibid., 2 July 1988, p. 10.
112 Ibid., p. 12.
113 Ibid., p. 1.
114 Ibid., 1 July 1988, pp. 8, 9; ibid., 2 July 1988, pp. 3, 4; and elsewhere.
115 Ibid., 30 June 1988, p. 3.
116 Ibid., p. 2.
117 Ibid., 2 July 1988, p. 4.
118 Ibid., 30 June 1988, p. 6.
119 Ibid., p. 7.
120 Ibid.
121 Ibid., p. 5.
122 Ibid., 2 July 1988, p. 4.
123 Ibid., p. 6; in respect of the Politburo in particular, ibid., 1 July 1988, p. 6.
124 Ibid., 30 June 1988, p. 4.
125 Ibid., 2 July 1988, p. 4.
126 Ibid., pp. 4, 6.
127 Ibid., pp. 9, 12.
128 Ibid., p. 4.
129 Ibid., 30 June 1988, p. 4, and 2 July 1988, p. 9.
130 Ibid., 1 July 1988, p. 6.
131 Ibid., 2 July 1988, p. 4.
132 Ibid., p. 8, and 1 July 1988, p. 9.
133 Ibid., 2 July 1988, p. 5.
134 Ibid., 30 June 1988, p. 5.

135 Ibid., p. 7, and 1 July 1988, p. 2.
136 Ibid., p. 9.
137 Ibid., 2 July 1988, p. 1.
138 Ibid., 5 July 1988, p. 2.
139 Ibid., 31 July 1988, p. 1.
140 Peter Reddaway, 'Resisting Gorbachev', *New York Review of Books*, 18 August 1988, p. 36.
141 Gill, *Rules*, pp. 173, 47, 63.
142 A. Solzhenitsyn, *Arkhipelag Gulag 1918–1956. Opyt khudozhestven-nogo issledovaniya*, parts 3 and 4 (Paris: YMCA Press, 1974), p. 293.
143 Vladimir Voinovich, *Antisovetskii Sovetskii Soyuz* (Ann Arbor: Ardis, 1985), p. 55.
144 As noted in Gill, *Rules*, p. 7.
145 *Pravda*, 10 February 1987, p. 2.
146 See, for instance, William E. Odom's reference to a 'purge of a new type' in his 'How Far Can Gorbachev Go?', *Problems of Communism*, vol. 36, no. 6 (November – December 1987), pp. 18–33, at p. 30.
147 *Pravda*, 29 June 1988, pp. 2–7.
148 See Jiri Pelikan (ed.), *The Secret Vysocany Congress* (London: Allen Lane, 1971), pp. 138, 140.
149 See William B. Simons and Stephen White (eds), *The Party Statutes of the Communist World* (The Hague: Martinus Nijhoff, 1984), p. 539, which contains the texts of both documents.

The Programme of the Communist Party of the Soviet Union
A New Edition

Approved by the 27th Congress of the CPSU on March 1, 1986

Introduction

Born of the Great October Socialist Revolution, the Soviet land has traversed a long and glorious road. Victories of worldwide historic importance have been scored under the leadership of the Communist Party. Consistently expressing the interests of the working class, of all working people, and armed with Marxist-Leninist teaching, with a wealth of experience in revolutionary struggle and the building of socialism, the CPSU is confidently leading the Soviet people along the course of communist creative endeavour and peace.

The Party emerged on the political scene as a worthy successor to the ideas of the socialist transformation of society proclaimed in the first programme document of the Communists – the *Communist Manifesto*, to the unfading exploit of the heroes of the Paris Commune, and to the revolutionary traditions of the international working class and of the Russian revolutionary democratic movement.

Relying on the historical experience of the class struggle and the best that was achieved by human thought, Karl Marx and Frederick Engels, founders of scientific communism, discovered the objective laws of social development, theoretically proved the inevitability of the collapse of capitalism, and substantiated the world historic mission of the proletariat as the creator of the new, communist system. Their passionate call – 'Workers of all countries, unite!' – remains to this day the fighting slogan of the working-class movement.

In new historical conditions Vladimir Ilyich Lenin, who brilliantly continued the cause of Marx and Engels, comprehensively developed their teaching, provided answers to vital questions of the times and armed the working-class movement with the theory of socialist revolution and the building of socialism, with a scientific system of views on problems of war and peace.

Marxism-Leninism is an integral revolutionary teaching. Created by the great Lenin, the Party has become the living embodiment of the fusion of scientific socialism with the working-class movement, of the unbreakable unity of theory and practice. It has been and will be a party of Marxism-Leninism, a party of revolutionary action.

At each stage in history the CPSU accomplished the tasks that were scientifically formulated in its programmes.

Having adopted its First Programme at the 2nd Congress in 1903, the Bolshevik Party led the working class, the peasantry, all the working people of Russia in the struggle to overthrow the tsarist autocracy and then the capitalist system, and passed through the flames of three Russian revolutions. In October 1917 the working class took political power into its hands. A state of workers and peasants came into being for the first time in history. **The creation of a new world began.**

In the Second Programme, adopted at the 8th Congress in 1919, the Party set the task of building socialism. Following untrodden paths, overcoming incredible difficulties, and displaying unprecedented heroism, the Soviet people under the leadership of the Communist Party implemented the plan for building socialism worked out by Lenin. **Socialism in our country became a reality.**

With the adoption of the Third Programme at the 22nd Congress in 1961, the Party undertook enormous work in all areas of the building of communism. The Soviet society achieved great successes in developing productive forces, economic and social relations, socialist democracy, and culture, and in moulding the new man. **The country entered the stage of developed socialism.** The role of the Soviet Union grew as a powerful factor in the struggle against the imperialist policy of oppression, aggression and war, for peace, democracy and social progress.

The time that has elapsed since the Third Programme was adopted has confirmed the correctness of its main theoretical and political propositions. At the same time, accumulated experience and scientific understanding of the changes in the country's domestic life and in the world arena provide an opportunity to define more accurately and concretely the prospects for Soviet society's development, the ways and means of attaining the ultimate goal – communism, and the tasks of international policy in new historical conditions.

The Third Programme of the CPSU in its present updated edition is a programme for the planned and all-round perfection of socialism, for Soviet society's further advance to communism through the country's accelerated socio-economic development. It is a programme of the struggle for peace and social progress.

Part One

The Transition from Capitalism to Socialism and Communism – The Main Content of the Present Epoch

I. The Great October Socialist Revolution and the Building of Socialism in the USSR

Mankind's history-making turn towards socialism, begun by the October Revolution, is a natural result of social development.

Capitalism is the last exploiter system in human history. Having given a powerful impetus to the development of productive forces, it then became an obstacle to social progress.

The history of capitalism is the history of the aggravation of its main contradiction – the contradiction between the social nature of production and the private capitalist form of appropriation, of the growing exploitation of the working class and all working people, of the aggravation of the struggle between labour and capital, the oppressed and the oppressors, of economic crises, socio-political upheavals, wars of conquest and conflicts bringing endless hardships to working people.

Early in the 20th century the process of the concentration and centralisation of capital resulted in the emergence of powerful capitalist monopoly associations that seized the main levers in the whole of economic and political life. Capitalism entered its highest and last stage – the stage of imperialism. In the words of Lenin, 'capitalism in its imperialist stage has turned into the greatest oppressor of nations', the primary source of wars of aggression.

The material conditions for replacing capitalist production relations by socialist ones took shape and the objective and subjective prerequisites for a victorious socialist revolution mature at the stage of imperialism. **History has entrusted the working class with the mission of the revolutionary transformation of the old society and the creation of the new one.** In fulfilling this mission the working class serves not just its own class interests, but those of all working people.

Aggravated by tsarist oppression and the vestiges of serfdom, imperialism's contradictions manifested themselves in Russia with exceptional force. Russia turned out to be the weakest link of world imperialism, the focal point of its contradictions. It was to Russia that the centre of the world revolutionary movement shifted, and the Russian proletariat faced the most difficult and important task of being the first to break the chain of the bourgeoisie's world domination. This could be done only under the leadership of a party of a new type – a fighting revolutionary organisation of the proletariat.

The formation of the Bolshevik Party became the turning point in the history of the Russian and international working-class movement. This was an expression of an objective requirement of social development, of the proletariat's class struggle, the fruit of scientific foresight, a result of the untiring political and organisational activity of Lenin and the Marxists who had rallied round him. Lenin's ardent call 'Give us an organisation of revolutionaries and we will overturn Russia' found fervent response in the hearts and minds of workers, the progressive-minded people in Russian society, the best representatives of the working people. Lenin worked out the ideological, political and organisational principles of the Party, and the methods for its work among the masses. The party of the new type was being formed and growing stronger in the course of implacable clashes with revisionism, right-wing opportunism, dogmatism and leftist adventurism.

The revolution of 1905–1907, the people's revolution of the imperialist epoch, showed the strength of the working class and was a prologue to the proletariat's coming victories. The bourgeois-democratic revolution of February 1917 eliminated tsarism, but it did not deliver the popular masses from social and national oppression, from the hardships of imperialist war, nor did it resolve the contradictions that were tearing Russian society apart. Socialist revolution became an urgent demand of the times.

The working class of Russia was known for its fervent revolutionary spirit and high level of organisation. It was led by the Bolshevik Party, steeled in political battles and armed with progressive revolutionary theory. Lenin gave it a clear perspective of struggle by evolving the theory that a victorious proletarian revolution in conditions of imperialism was possible initially in one or several countries.

At the call of the Bolshevik Party and under its leadership the working class began a decisive battle against the power of capital. The Party brought together into one powerful stream the proletarian struggle for socialism, the peasants' struggle for land, the national liberation struggle of Russia's oppressed peoples, and the nationwide movement against imperialist war and for peace, and directed that stream towards overthrowing the bourgeois system.

The Great October Socialist Revolution became a landmark in world history, determined the general direction and main trends of world development, and initiated the irreversible process of the replacement of capitalism by the new, communist socio-economic formation.

A state with the dictatorship of the proletariat emerged and became established for the first time in history. Rallying together all working people, the working class set about resolving the most complex problems of the period of transition from capitalism to socialism, and creating the foundations of the new society.

The winning of political power, victories on the Civil War fronts, the rout of foreign military interventionists, and prospects for building a new life generated a powerful upsurge of strength and revolutionary energy among the working people. They overcame the privations and difficulties caused by economic dislocation, the counterrevolutionary plots and sabotage by the bourgeoisie, and the country's technical, economic and cultural backwardness. In the transition period the class struggle at times took the form of bitter clashes. The Soviet Union was subjected to fierce attacks by the hostile capitalist encirclement, to numerous military and political provocations.

Relying on the enthusiasm of the masses, repulsing the attacks by right-wing and leftist opportunists, and strengthening its ideological, political and organisational unity, the Party undeviatingly pursued the Leninist general line aimed at building socialism.

The basic means of production passed into the hands of the people. The **nationalisation** of land, factories, plants and banks ensured the preconditions necessary for asserting and developing socialist ownership and organising a system of planned economy. **Industrialisation** turned the Soviet Union into a powerful industrial state. **Collectivisation** of agriculture was a breakthrough in economic relations, in the entire life of the peasantry. The alliance of the working class and the peasantry was placed on a solid socio-economic foundation. As a result of the **cultural revolution,** illiteracy was stamped out, broad vistas were opened for the development of creative forces and the intellectual flourishing of the working man, a socialist intelligentsia emerged, and Marxist-Leninist ideology became dominant in the minds of the Soviet people.

The solution of the **nationalities question** is an outstanding accomplishment of socialism. The victory of the October Revolution forever put an end to national oppression and inequality among nations and ethnic groups. A tremendous role was played here by the voluntary unification of the free and equal peoples into a single multinational state – the Union of Soviet Socialist Republics. In the course of building socialism rapid economic, social and cultural progress of the former national outlands was ensured. Ethnic conflicts became a thing of the past, and fraternal friendship, close cooperation and mutual assistance of all peoples of the USSR became a way of life.

All this signified that a social transformation of worldwide historic importance had been accomplished – the age-old dominance of private ownership was eliminated and exploitation of man by man abolished forever. Socio-political and ideological unity of Soviet society took shape on the basis of the common interests of the working class, the collective farmers, people's intelligentsia, and the working people of all nationalities. The working man became the full master of the country. **A socialist society in the USSR was essentially built.**

The Great Patriotic War was a severe trial for the new system. The Soviet people and its armed forces rallied round the Party and, displaying unprecedented heroism, inflicted a crushing defeat on German fascism – the strike force of world imperialist reaction. By its victory the Soviet Union made the decisive contribution to the liberation of European peoples from Nazi slavery, to saving world civilisation. The rout of Nazi Germany and militarist Japan opened up new possibilities for peoples' struggle for peace, democracy, national liberation and socialism. The Soviet people's victory raised high the Soviet state's international prestige.

Within a short period the USSR healed the deep wounds of war, considerably strengthened its economic, scientific, technological and defence potential, and consolidated its position internationally. **The victory of socialism in our country was final and complete.**

In its economic, socio-political and cultural development, Soviet society, relying on its achievements, continued to advance confidently. An integral national economic complex took shape in the country. Large new areas in the North and East of the country were developed, and nature management became more efficient. National income and productivity of social labour grew considerably. The level of the people's well-being was raised substantially and a huge housing construction programme was carried out. The people's cultural wealth increased, the transition to universal secondary education was completed, and Soviet science and technology achieved outstanding successes. The Soviet Union built the first atomic power station and the first atomic-powered ice-breaker; it also launched the first artificial satellite of the Earth and the first manned spaceship.

The socialist social relations gained in strength, a new social and international community – the Soviet people – emerged. The state with the dictatorship of the proletariat grew into a socialist state of all people.

Displaying Bolshevist fidelity to principle and a self-critical approach, and relying on the support of the masses, the Party did a great deal to eliminate the consequences of the personality cult, deviations from the Leninist norms of party and state guidance, and to rectify errors of a subjectivist, voluntaristic nature. Soviet democracy was further developed and socialist legality consolidated.

The Soviet people's persistent work, great achievements in the economic, social and political spheres, science and culture have brought our country to new historical frontiers that marked the beginning of the stage of developed socialism.

The establishment of military-strategic parity between the USSR and the USA, between the Warsaw Treaty Organisation and NATO was a historic accomplishment of socialism. It strengthened the positions of the USSR, the countries of socialism and all progressive forces, and dashed the hopes cherished by aggressive imperialist circles of winning a world nuclear war. Preservation of this balance is vital for ensuring peace and international security.

The experience of the USSR and other socialist countries convincingly demonstrates the indisputable socio-economic, political, ideological and moral advantages of the new society as a stage in mankind's progress that is superior to capitalism, and provides answers to questions that the bourgeois system is incapable of solving.

Socialism is a society on whose banner are inscribed the words 'Everything for the sake of man, everything for the benefit of man'. It is a society in which:

– the means of production are in the hands of the people, an end has been put forever to exploitation of man by man, social oppression, the rule of a privileged minority, and the poverty and illiteracy of millions of people;
– the broadest vistas have been opened for the dynamic and planned development of productive forces, and scientific and technological progress brings not unemployment but a steady growth in the well-being of the entire people;
– the equal right to work and pay in conformity with the principle 'From each according to his ability, to each according to his work' is ensured, and the population enjoys such social benefits as free medical service and education, and housing with a minimum rent;
– the inviolable alliance of the working class, the collective

farmers and intelligentsia has been affirmed, men and women have
equal rights and guarantees for exercising them, the young generation is offered a reliable road into the future, and social security for
veterans of labour is guaranteed;
    – national inequality is abolished, the juridical and factual
equality, friendship and brotherhood of all peoples and nationalities
are established;
    – genuine democracy – power exercised for the people and by the
people – has been established and is developing, and broad and
equal participation of citizens in the management of production,
public and state affairs is ensured;
    – the ideas of freedom, human rights and dignity of the individual
are filled with real content, unity of rights and duties is ensured,
uniform laws and norms of morality and a single discipline apply to
each and all, and increasingly favourable conditions are taking shape
for all-round development of the individual;
    – the truly humanistic Marxist-Leninist ideology is dominant, the
popular masses have access to all sources of knowledge, and an
advanced socialist culture has been created which absorbs all that is
best in world culture;
    – a socialist way of life which gives working people confidence
in the future, spiritually and morally elevates them as creators of
new social relations and of their own destiny has taken shape on the
basis of social justice, collectivism and comradely mutual assistance.

Socialism is a society whose deeds and intentions in the international
arena are directed towards supporting the peoples' striving for
independence and social progress, and are subordinated to the main
task of preserving and consolidating peace.
    At the new stage of historical development our Party and the
Soviet people are faced with the task in all its magnitude of the all-
round perfection of socialist society and a fuller and more effective
utilisation of its possibilities and advantages for further advance
towards communism.

II. Struggle Between the Forces of Progress and Reaction in the Modern World

After the rout of German fascism and Japanese militarism the
worldwide historical process of social liberation, which began with
the Great October Revolution, was marked by the overthrow of the
power of exploiters in several countries in Europe and Asia and then
America. **Socialism, which first became a reality in our country,
has turned into a world system.** The Marxist-Leninist theory of

building the new society has been verified in practice on an international scale, socialism has asserted itself on vast expanses of the earth, and hundreds of millions of people are following the road of creating a communist civilisation. More and more nations are losing their confidence in capitalism; they do not wish to associate their prospects of development with it and are persistently searching for and finding ways of socialist transformation of their countries.

The successes of socialism are all the more impressive because they have been achieved within very short time spans, in conditions of imperialism's unceasing pressure – from economic pressure and ideological subversion to direct attempts to stage counterrevolutionary coups and launch military aggression.

The experience accumulated in socialist countries is of lasting significance. The past decades have enriched the practice of the building of socialism and clearly demonstrated the diversity of the world of socialism. At the same time the experience of these decades shows the immense importance of the **general laws of socialism**, such as: the power of working people, with the working class playing the leading role; guidance of society's development by the Communist Party armed with the ideology of scientific socialism; establishment of social ownership of the basic means of production and on this basis the planned growth of the economy in the interests of the people; implementation of the principle 'From each according to his ability, to each according to his work'; development of socialist democracy; equality and friendship of all nations and nationalities; and defence of revolutionary gains from encroachments by class enemies.

The use of the general laws in the specific conditions of each of the socialist countries forms the basis of their confident advance, the overcoming of the growing pains and the resolving in good time of contradictions that arise; it is a real contribution of the ruling Communist parties to the general process of socialist development.

Socialism has brought forth a new, previously unknown type of international relations, which are developing between socialist states. Their firm foundation consists of a uniform socio-economic and political system; Marxist-Leninist ideology; class solidarity; friendship, cooperation and mutual assistance in carrying out tasks of building and defending the new society; the struggle for peace, international security, social progress; and equality and respect for the independence and sovereignty of each state.

Relations of socialist internationalism have been most fully embodied in the **socialist community**. The countries belonging to the community – member states of the Council for Mutual Economic Assistance and the Warsaw Treaty Organisation – are united by common fundamental interests and aims and by ties of extensive multifaceted cooperation, and coordinate their actions in international affairs. History has not known such a community of countries in which no one country has or can have special rights and privileges, in which international relations have really become relations between peoples, and in which fruitful ties at various levels have taken shape and are developing – from the highest level of Party and state leadership to work collectives. The community multiplies the strength of the fraternal states in the building of socialism and helps reliably to ensure their security.

The objective requirement of the socialist countries' drawing ever closer together stems from the very essence of socialism. Whereas in the capitalist world the law of uneven economic, socio-political and cultural development operates, and strong countries enrich themselves by plundering weak ones and prolong in every way the backwardness of the latter, socialism creates the necessary conditions for raising the less developed countries to the level of the developed ones. The higher and the more similar the levels of social development of socialist countries, the richer and deeper their cooperation, the more organic the process of their drawing together.

The establishment of the world socialist system, the formation and strengthening of the socialist community have brought about a **fundamental change in the alignment of forces in the international arena** in favour of the peoples fighting for social progress, democracy, national freedom and peace. The socialist community is the most authoritative force of our time and without it no issue in world politics can be solved; it is a firm bulwark of peace on earth, the most consistent champion of sound, peaceful, democratic principles in international relations, the main force opposing imperialist reaction.

The young, forward-looking world of socialism is opposed by the exploiter world of capitalism which is still strong and dangerous, but which has already passed its peak. **The general crisis of capitalism is deepening**. The sphere of its domination is shrinking inevitably, its historical doom becoming ever more obvious.

Modern capitalism differs in many ways from what it was at the beginning and even in the middle of the 20th century. In conditions of state-monopoly capitalism, which combines the strength of the monopolies and the state, the conflict between the vastly increased productive forces and capitalist production relations is becoming ever more acute. The inner instability of the economy is growing, which is seen in the slowing down of the overall rates of its growth, in the intertwining and deepening of cyclical and structural crises. Mass unemployment and inflation have become a chronic disease, and budget deficits and state debts have reached a colossal scale.

The strengthening of transnational corporations, which make huge profits by exploiting working people on a world scale, is a direct result of capitalist concentration and internationalisation of production. They not only undermine the sovereignty of newly free states, but also encroach on the national interests of developed capitalist countries.

The monopoly bourgeoisie is constantly manoeuvring in an attempt to adjust itself to the changing situation. A capitalist state redistributes, in particular through the budget, a considerable part of the national income in favour of big capital and tries to place at its service the latest achievements in science and technology. The mechanism of exploitation has become more complex, more sophisticated. The skills, intellectual powers and the energy of the worker are being exploited for gaining more and more profit.

With the growing influence of world socialism, the class struggle of working people at times compels the capitalists to make partial concessions, to agree to certain improvements as regards working conditions, remuneration for work and social security. This is being done to preserve the main thing – the domination of capital. Such manoeuvring, however, is being increasingly combined with violent actions, with a direct assault by the monopolies and the bourgeois state on the living standards of working people.

Under capitalism the scientific and technological revolution has grave social consequences. Millions of working people, thrown out of the factory gates, are doomed to losing their skills and to material hardships, and can have no confidence in the future. A considerable proportion of young people cannot find application for their energy and knowledge and suffer from the hopelessness of their condition. Mass unemployment remains regardless of the economic situation, while the real prospect of its further growth is fraught with the most serious upheavals for capitalism as a social system.

The monopolies have seized the dominant positions in the agrarian sector of the economy. Large numbers of farmers are being forced out of the production sphere while those who survive do so at the cost of excessive work and privations. The fate of farmers' families depends entirely on market fluctuations and the arbitrariness of monopolies. The plight of the peasantry is especially grave in the former colonies and semi-colonies. The small and middle businessmen in cities are being increasingly exploited by big capital and are caught in the net of financial dependence.

Even in the most developed capitalist countries a great number of people are deprived, homeless, illiterate and without medical care. Shameful discrimination against ethnic minorities persists and the rights of women are infringed upon.

A tendency towards an all-round intensification of reaction is characteristic of imperialism in the political field. Wherever the working people have achieved certain democratic rights as a result of determined struggle, state-monopoly capitalism is conducting a persistent, at times cunningly camouflaged offensive against those rights. In situations that pose a danger to state-monopoly capitalism, it resorts without hesitation to political blackmail, repression, terror and punitive actions. Neo-fascism is becoming increasingly active in the political arena. When the usual forms of suppressing working people fail, imperialism implants and backs tyrannic regimes in order directly to suppress progressive forces by military means. Striving to weaken the international solidarity of working people, imperialism stirs up and abets national egoism, chauvinism and racism, and scorn for the rights and interests of other peoples and their national cultural and historical heritage.

The inhumane ideology of modern capitalism is inflicting every great damage on the spiritual world of people. The cult of individualism, violence and permissiveness, rabid anti-communism and exploitation of culture as a source of profit give rise to spiritual callousness, to moral degradation. Imperialism has given rise to large-scale crime and terrorism that have engulfed capitalist society. Ever more pernicious is the role of the bourgeois mass media which befuddle people in the interest of the ruling class.

The uneven nature of the development of countries within the capitalist system is deepening. Three main centres of inter-imperialist rivalry have formed: the United States, Western Europe and Japan. Competition is mounting between them for markets, spheres of capital investment, sources of raw materials and superiority in the key areas of scientific and technological progress. New centres of economic and political rivalry are forming, particularly in the Pacific basin and in Latin America. Contradictions between bourgeois states are deepening. The imperial ambitions and selfish policy of the US monopolies and their readiness, for egoistic reasons, to sacrifice the interests and security of other, even allied, states are giving rise to growing indignation and alarm throughout the world.

Imperialism is responsible for the huge and widening gap between the economic development levels of the industrial capitalist countries and the majority of the newly free states, for the continued existence on earth of vast zones of hunger, poverty and epidemic diseases.

As the course of historical development more and more weakens the positions of imperialism, the policy of its more reactionary forces becomes increasingly hostile to the interests of the peoples. Imperialism is putting up fierce resistance to social progress, and is trying to stop the course of history, to undermine the positions of socialism, and to avenge itself socially on a world scale. The imperialist powers strive to coordinate their economic, political and ideological strategy, to create a common front of struggle against socialism, against all revolutionary, liberation movements.

Imperialism refuses to face the political realities of today's world. Ignoring the will of sovereign peoples, it tries to deprive them of their right to choose their road of development and threatens their security. Herein lies the main cause of conflicts in various parts of the world.

The citadel of international reaction is US imperialism. The threat of war comes chiefly from it. Claiming world domination, it arbitrarily declares whole continents to be zones of its 'vital interests'. The US policy of hegemony, the imposition of its will and unequal relations on other states, support for repressive anti-popular regimes and discrimination against countries that do not suit the United States, disorganises inter-state economic and political relations and prevents their normal development.

The bloody war against Vietnam, the blockade of Cuba for many years, the flouting of the lawful rights of the Palestinian people, the intervention in Lebanon, the armed seizure of defenceless Grenada, and the aggressive actions against Nicaragua – these are only some of the countless crimes that will remain forever the most shameful pages in imperialism's history.

The race unleashed by imperialism in the manufacture of nuclear and other arms on a scale that knows no precedent is its gravest crime against the peoples. It brings the monopolies huge profits. The colossal military expenditures weigh heavily on the shoulders of working people. The monopolies that manufacture arms, the military, the state bureaucracy, the ideological machinery and militarised science, that have merged to form the military-industrial complex, have become the most zealous advocates and makers of policies of adventurism and aggression. The sinister alliance of the death merchants and imperialist state power is a pillar of extreme reaction, a constant and growing source of war danger, and a convincing confirmation of the capitalist system's political social and moral untenability.

No 'modifications' and manoeuvres by modern capitalism have rendered invalid or can render invalid the laws of its development, or can overcome the acute antagonism between labour and capital, between the monopolies and society, or can bring the historically doomed capitalist system out of its all-permeating crisis. The dialectics of development are such that the very same means which capitalism puts to use with the aim of strengthening its positions inevitably lead to an aggravation of all its deep-seated contradictions. Imperialism is parasitical, decaying and moribund capitalism; it marks the eve of socialist revolution.

The working class was and is the main revolutionary class of the present age. In the capitalist world, it is the main force struggling for the overthrow of the exploiting system and for building a new society.

Practice confirms the Marxist-Leninist concept of the increasing role of the working class in society. As science is being applied in production on an ever larger scale, the ranks of the working class are being replenished with highly skilled workers. In the course of class battles, the working class becomes more cohesive, creates its own political parties, trade unions and other organisations, and wages economic, political and ideological struggle against capitalism. The scale of that struggle is growing, its forms are becoming more diverse and its content is being enriched. The basic interests of the proletariat make it more and more imperative to achieve unity in the working-class movement and concerted actions by all its contingents.

The young and rapidly growing working class in the countries of Asia, Africa and Latin America is facing difficult tasks. It is opposed both by foreign capital and local exploiters. Its political maturity and degree of organisation are growing in the course of struggle.

The vanguard of the working-class movement, of all the forces of the world revolutionary process is the international communist movement. Communists are working for both the immediate and the long-term goals of the working class, for the interests of all the working people, for social progress, national liberation of peoples, disarmament and peace. The communist movement is the most influential ideological and political force of our time.

The revolutionary parties of the working class are guided by the scientific theory of social development, Marxism-Leninism, and are pursuing a principled working-class policy. They are characterised by a conviction in the historical inevitability of the replacement of capitalism by socialism, a clear understanding of the objective laws of socialist revolution in whatever form – peaceful or non-peaceful – and an ability to apply the general principles of struggle for socialism in the specific conditions of every country.

The strength of revolutionary parties lies in the fact that they firmly uphold the rights and vital aspirations of the working people, point out ways of leading society out of the crisis situation of bourgeois society, indicate a real alternative to the exploiter system and provide answers, imbued with social optimism, to the basic questions of our time. They are the true exponents and the most staunch defenders of the national interests of their countries.

A consistently class-oriented course enhances the authority of the Communist parties, despite the fact that the political and ideological machinery of imperialism is operating in an increasingly subtle way. It is combining discrimination against and persecution of Communists and outright anti-communist propaganda with support for those elements in the working-class movement that are opposed to working-class policy and international solidarity, and that endorse social reconciliation and partnership with the bourgeoisie. The monopoly bourgeoisie and reactionary forces attack the Communists so fiercely precisely because the latter represent a movement that has deep roots in social development and that expresses the most vital interests of the mass of the people.

A characteristic feature of our time is **an upsurge of mass democratic movements in the non-socialist world**. The antagonism between the monopolies and the overwhelming majority of the population is deepening in capitalist countries. Professionals and office employees, farmers, representatives of the urban petty bourgeoisie and national minorities, women's organisations, young people and students are taking an ever more active part in the struggle against the dominance of the monopolies and against the reactionary policy of the ruling classes. People of different political views are demanding an end to the militarisation of society and to the policy of aggression and war, an end to racial and national discrimination, to infringements on the rights of women, to the deterioration in the condition of the younger generation, to corruption, and to the predatory attitude of the monopolies towards the use of natural resources and the environment. These movements are objectively directed against the policy of the reactionary circles of imperialism and merge with the overall struggle for peace and social progress.

The anti-imperialist struggle of the peoples and countries that have cast off the yoke of colonialism for the consolidation of their independence and for social progress is an integral part of the world revolutionary process. The disintegration of the colonial system of imperialism and the emergence of dozens of independent states from its ruins are an historic achievement of the national liberation revolutions and movements, an achievement that has considerably influenced the alignment of forces in the world.

Since independence many of those countries have made appreciable progress in economic and cultural development and in consolidating national statehood. Collective forms of struggle by those countries for their rights in the international arena have taken shape. Practice has shown, however, that their way to the consolidation of political independence and to economic and social rejuvenation is being seriously hampered by the legacy of their colonial and semi-colonial past and by the actions of imperialism.

Conducting a policy of neo-colonialism, imperialism is seeking to reduce to naught the sovereignty won by the young states and to retain and even tighten control over them. It is trying to drag them into a militarist orbit and to use them as springboards for its aggressive global strategy. In pursuing these goals, the imperialists resort to military pressure, impose their economic diktat and support internal reaction. Even countries that won state independence long ago, for instance, Latin American countries, have to wage a resolute struggle against the dominance of the monopolies of the United States and other imperialist powers.

Taking advantage of the economic and technological dependence of the newly free countries and their unequal status in the world capitalist economy, imperialism mercilessly exploits them. It is exacting tributes that run into billions of dollars, and which are exhausting the economies of those states. The huge indebtedness of the countries of Asia, Africa and Latin America to the industrially developed capitalist states has become an important lever for the exploitation of these countries by imperialism, and primarily US imperialism. At the same time, the resistance of the peoples of these countries to the policy of plunder and robbery is growing. They are continuing their determined, just struggle against neo-colonialism, against interference in their internal affairs, and against racism and apartheid. This resistance objectively links up with the overall anti-imperialist struggle of the peoples for freedom, peace, and social progress.

The non-capitalist way of development, **the way of socialist orientation**, chosen by a number of newly free countries, is opening up broad prospects for social progress. The experience of these countries confirms that in present-day conditions, with the existing world alignment of forces, the formerly enslaved peoples have greater possibilities for rejecting capitalism and for building their future without exploiters, in the interests of the working people. This is a phenomenon of immense historic importance.

Overcoming the resistance of external and internal reaction, the ruling revolutionary-democratic parties are pursuing a course of abolishing the dominance of imperialist monopolies, tribal chiefs, feudal lords and the reactionary bourgeoisie; of strengthening the public sector of the economy; of encouraging the cooperative movement in the countryside; and of enhancing the role of the mass of the working people in economic and political life. Defending their independence against the onslaught of the imperialists, these countries are broadening their cooperation with socialist states. The road chosen by them meets the genuine interests and aspirations of the mass of the people, reflects their desire for a just social system, and coincides with the mainstream of historical development.

The most acute problem facing mankind is that of war and peace. Imperialism was responsible for two world wars that claimed tens of millions of lives. It is creating the threat of a third world war. Imperialism is using the achievements of man's genius for the development of weapons of awesome destructive power. The policy of the imperialist circles, which are prepared to sacrifice the future of whole nations, is increasing the danger that these weapons may actually be put to use. In the final count it threatens mankind with a global armed conflict in which there would be no winners or losers and in which world civilisation could perish.

The question of what goals the achievements of the scientific and technological revolution should serve has become pivotal in the present-day socio-political struggle. Contemporary science and technology make it possible to ensure abundance on earth and to create material conditions for the flourishing of society and the development of the individual. These creations of the human mind and human hands, however, are being turned against humanity itself owing to class selfishness, for the sake of the enrichment of the elite, which dominates the capitalist world. This is a glaring contradiction which confronts mankind as it approaches the threshold of the 21st century.

It is not science and technology in themselves that pose a threat to peace. This threat is posed by imperialism and its policy, the policy of the most reactionary militarist, aggressive forces of our time. The threat can be averted only by curbing those forces.

In the present-day world, which is riddled with acute contradictions, and in the face of impending catastrophe, the only sensible and acceptable way out is **the peaceful coexistence of states with different social systems.** This does not merely mean the absence of wars. It is an international order under which good-neighbourliness and cooperation rather than armed force would prevail, and a broad exchange of the achievements of science and technology and cultural values would be carried out for the good of all nations. When vast resources are no longer used for military purposes, it would be possible to use the fruits of labour exclusively for constructive purposes. States that have embarked on the road of independent development would be protected from external encroachments, and this would facilitate their advance along the path of national and social revival. Favourable opportunities would also arise for solving the global problems by the collective efforts of all states. Peaceful coexistence meets the interests of all countries and peoples.

The danger looming over mankind has never been so awesome. But then the possibilities for safeguarding and strengthening peace have never been so real. By uniting their efforts the peoples can and must avert the threat of nuclear annihilation.

The aggressive policy of imperialism is being countered by the growing potential of the forces of peace. This means the vigorous and consistently peaceful policy of the socialist states and their growing economic and defensive capacity. This means the policy of the overwhelming majority of states of Asia, Africa and Latin America which have a vital interest in safeguarding peace and ending the arms race. This means the anti-war movements of the broadest mass of the people on all continents, movements that have become a long-lasting and influential factor in the life of society. A realistic assessment of the actual alignment of forces is leading many statesmen and politicians in capitalist states, too, to an understanding of the danger involved in continuing and extending the arms race.

The CPSU proceeds from the belief that, however grave the threat to peace posed by the policy of the aggressive circles of imperialism, **world war is not fatally inevitable. It is possible to avert war and to save mankind from catastrophe. This is the historical mission of socialism, of all the progressive and peace-loving forces of the world.**

The entire course of world development confirms the Marxist-Leninist analysis of the character and main content of the present epoch. **It is an epoch of transition from capitalism to socialism and communism, and of historical competition between the two world socio-political systems, an epoch of socialist and national liberation revolutions and of the disintegration of colonialism, an epoch of struggle of the main motive forces of social development – world socialism, the working-class and communist movement, the peoples of the newly free states, and the mass democratic movements – against imperialism and its policy of aggression and oppression, and for peace, democracy, and social progress.**

The constant growth of these forces and their interaction are a pledge that the hopes of the peoples for a life of peace, freedom, and happiness will be fulfilled. The advance of humanity towards socialism and communism, despite all its unevenness, complexity and contradictoriness, is inevitable.

58

Part Two

The CPSU's Tasks in Perfecting Socialism and Making a Gradual Transition to Communism

I. The Communist Perspective of the USSR and the Need to Accelerate Social and Economic Development

The ultimate goal of the CPSU is to build communism in our country. Socialism and communism are two consecutive phases of one communist formation. There is no distinct line dividing them: the development of socialism, an ever fuller revelation and use of its possibilities and advantages, and the consolidation of the general communist principles characteristic of it – this is what is meant by the actual advance of society to communism.

Communism is a classless social system with one form of public ownership of the means of production and with full social equality of all members of society. Under communism, the all-round development of people will be accompanied by the growth of the productive forces on the basis of continuous progress in science and technology, all the springs of social wealth will flow abundantly, and the great principle 'From each according to his ability, to each according to his needs' will be implemented. Communism is a highly organised society of free, socially conscious working people, a society in which public self-government will be established, a society in which labour for the good of society will become the prime vital requirement of everyone, a clearly recognised necessity, and the ability of each person will be employed to the greatest benefit of the people.

The material and technical foundation of communism presupposes the creation of those productive forces that open up opportunities for the full satisfaction of the reasonable requirements of society and the individual. All productive activities under communism will be based on the use of highly efficient technical facilities and technologies, and the harmonious interaction of man and nature will be ensured.

In the highest phase of communism the directly social character of labour and production will become firmly established. Through the complete elimination of the remnants of the old division of labour and the essential social differences associated with it, the process of forming a socially homogeneous society will be completed.

Communism signifies the transformation of the system of socialist self-government by the people, of socialist democracy into the highest form of organisation of society – communist public self-government. With the maturation of the necessary socio-economic and ideological preconditions and the involvement of all citizens in administration, the socialist state – given appropriate international conditions – will, as Lenin noted, increasingly become a transitional form 'from a state to a non-state'. The activities of state bodies will become non-political in nature, and the need for the state as a special political institution will gradually disappear.

The inalienable feature of the communist mode of life is a high level of consciousness, social activity, discipline, and self-discipline of members of society, in which observance of the uniform, generally accepted rules of communist conduct will become an inner need and habit of every person.

Communism is a social system under which the free development of each is a condition for the free development of all.

The CPSU does not attempt to foresee in detail the features of complete communism. As society advances towards communism and more experience is accumulated in building it, scientific notions of the highest phase of a new society will become enriched and more concrete.

The growth of socialism into communism is determined by the objective laws of the development of society, laws which cannot be disregarded. Any attempts to move ahead too fast and to introduce communist principles without taking into consideration the level of material and spiritual maturity of society are, as experience has shown, doomed to failure and may cause both economic and political losses.

At the same time, the CPSU believes that there must be no delay in effecting the necessary transformations and solving new tasks. The Party takes into account the fact that along with undeniable successes the 1970s and early 1980s saw certain unfavourable trends and difficulties in the country's development. To a great extent these were due to the failure to assess appropriately and in good time changes in the economic situation and the need for profound transformations in all spheres of life, and to a lack of persistence in carrying them out. This prevented fuller use of the possibilities and advantages of the socialist system and impeded onward movement.

The CPSU believes that under the present domestic and international conditions, the all-round progress of Soviet society, its onward movement towards communism can and must be ensured by **accelerating the country's socio-economic development**. This is the strategic line of the Party aimed at qualitatively transforming all aspects of life in Soviet society: a radical renewal of its material and technical foundation on the basis of the achievements of the scientific and technological revolution; perfection of social relations, above all economic ones; profound changes in the content and nature of labour and in the material and cultural conditions of the life of people; and invigoration of the entire system of political, social, and ideological institutions.

The Party links the successful solution of the tasks set with an **increase in the role of the human factor**. Socialist society cannot function effectively without finding new ways of developing the creative activity of the people in all spheres of life. The greater the scope of the historical goals, the more important the interested, responsible, conscious and active participation of millions of people in achieving them.

Soviet society is to reach new heights on the basis of accelerating its social and economic development. This means:

in the economic sphere – raising the national economy to a basically new scientific-technological and organisational-economic level, gearing it towards intensive development; achieving the world's highest level in productivity of social labour, quality of output, and efficiency of production; ensuring an optimal structure and balance for the integral national economic complex of the country; significantly raising the level of the socialisation of labour and production; drawing collective-farm and cooperative property and the property of the people as a whole closer together, with the prospect of their merging in future;

in the social sphere – ensuring a qualitatively new level of people's well-being while consistently implementing the socialist principle of distribution according to work; the establishment of an essentially classless structure of society, the gradual elimination of substantial differences in the socio-economic, cultural, and living standards of town and countryside; an ever more organic combination of physical and mental labour in production activities; further cohesion of the Soviet people as a social and international community; a high level of creative energy and initiative on the part of the masses;

in the political sphere – the development of socialist self-government by the people through ever greater involvement of citizens in running state and public affairs, the perfection of the electoral system, the improvement of the activities of elective bodies of people's power, the enhancement of the role of the trade unions, Komsomol, and other mass organisations of the working people, and an effective use of all forms of representative and direct democracy;

in the sphere of cultural life – the further consolidation of socialist ideology in the minds of Soviet people; full establishment of the moral principles of socialism, of the spirit of collectivism and comradely mutual assistance; bringing the achievements of science and cultural values within the reach of the broadest masses of the population; moulding a harmoniously developed man.

These transformations will bring about a qualitatively new state of Soviet society, which will fully reveal the enormous advantages of socialism in all spheres of life. Thus a historic step will be made on the road to the highest phase of communism. The Party always correlates its policy, economic and social strategy, and the tasks of its organisational and ideological work with the communist perspective.

II. The Economic Strategy of the Party

The task set by the Party to accelerate the social and economic development of the country calls for profound changes primarily in the decisive sphere of human activity – the economy. A sharp turn is to be made towards the intensification of production; every enterprise and every sector is to be reoriented towards the utmost and top-priority use of qualitative factors of economic growth. A transition must be ensured to an economy of supreme organisation and efficiency with comprehensively developed productive forces and production relations, and a smoothly functioning economic mechanism. The country's production potential should double and be renewed fundamentally and qualitatively by the year 2000.

These tasks are being tackled by the Party and the people under the conditions of the further development of the scientific and technological revolution, which is exerting strong influence on all aspects of present-day production, on the entire system of social relations, on man and his environment, and is opening up new prospects for considerably raising labour productivity and for the progress of society as a whole. The historical mission of socialism is to apply the achievements of science, the most advanced and efficient technology, and the growing force of people's creative and collective labour in the building of communism.

Acceleration of Scientific and Technological Progress – the Main Lever for Raising Efficiency in Production

The basic issue in the Party's economic strategy is the acceleration of scientific and technological progress. **A new technical reconstruction of the national economy is to be carried out** and the material and technical foundation of society thereby transformed.

Of primary importance is a rapid **renewal of the production apparatus through extensive introduction of advanced technology,** of the most advanced technological processes and flexible production lines that make it possible quickly to put out new products with maximum economic and social effect. It is necessary to complete comprehensive mechanisation in all sectors of the production and non-production spheres and to take a major step to promote the automation of production, involving a transition to automated shops and enterprises and automated control and design systems. Electrification, chemicalisation, robotisation, and computerisation of production will be effected and biotechnology used on an increasingly large scale.

The Party will facilitate in every way the further growth and effective use of the country's **scientific and technological potential** and the development of scientific research which opens up new opportunities for major, revolutionary changes in the intensification of the economy. The introduction of the latest achievements of science and technology in production, management, public services, and everyday life must be ensured everywhere. Science will become in full measure a force directly involved in production.

A considerable **increase in labour productivity** is to be achieved on the basis of accelerating scientific and technological progress, radical changes in machinery and technology, and mobilisation of all technical, organisational, economic and social factors. Without this, as Lenin taught, 'the full transition to communism is impossible'. Labour productivity is to be increased by 130–150 per cent in the coming fifteen years as an important stage on the way to the highest productivity.

Reserves for growth in labour productivity must be used to the utmost at every association, every enterprise, and every work-place. It is necessary to reduce the labour intensity of products, to cut the waste of working time, to introduce up-to-date machinery and technology, strengthen order and discipline, improve norm-setting, broadly apply advanced forms of scientific organisation of labour, raise production standards, make work collectives more stable, and encourage the efforts of inventors and innovators.

Scientific and technological progress should be aimed at a radical improvement in the **utilisation of natural resources, raw and other materials, fuel and energy** at all stages – from extracting and comprehensive processing of raw materials to the output and use of end products. The rates of reduction of material intensity, metal intensity and power intensity per unit of national income must be increased. Saving of resources will become the decisive means of meeting the increase in the requirements of the national economy in fuel, energy, and raw and other materials.

Utmost **improvement in the technical level and quality of products** is at the centre of the Party's economic policy and all practical work. Soviet products should incorporate the latest achievements of scientific thought, meet the highest technical, economic, aesthetic and other consumer demands, and be competitive on the world market. Improving product quality is a reliable way of more fully meeting the country's requirements in commodities and the population's growing demand for a variety of goods. Poor quality and rejects mean wasted material resources and labour. The Party will actively support efforts to maintain the reputation of the Soviet trade mark. The quality of products should be a matter of professional and patriotic pride.

The effectiveness of scientific and technological progress depends not only on an increase in the output of the latest technical facilities, but also on the **better use of fixed assets**, and an increase in the output of products per unit of equipment, per square metre of production space. The present downward trend in output-assets ratio is to be overcome, and in the long run this ratio is to be increased.

Accelerated scientific and technological progress is making greater demands on the general and vocational education of working people. The course of improving the entire system of training personnel and raising its skills, of ensuring, on a planned basis, a balance between the number of work-places and manpower resources in all economic sectors and regions of the country will be pursued.

The drive for all-round intensification and rationalisation of production, for its highest efficiency on the basis of scientific and technological progress is being organically combined, under the socialist system of planned economy, with the implementation of the humanitarian goals of Soviet society, with full employment and the steady improvement of all aspects of life.

Structural Reorganisation of Social Production

The switchover to intensification calls for serious **structural changes in the economy**. The national economy should be able to change flexibly and promptly in line with advances in science and technology, in social and individual requirements. There must be faster development of sectors essential for scientific and technological progress and for the successful solution of social tasks, an optimal correlation between consumption and accumulation, and a better balance between the manufacture of the means of production and consumer goods, between sectors in the agro-industrial complex. The social orientation of the economy will be strengthened and a turn will be made consistently to assure a more complete satisfaction of the Soviet people's growing requirements.

In this connection new demands are being made on **investment policy**. It is being called upon to ensure a higher effectiveness of capital investments, their concentration in the key sections that are essential for the prompt achievement of the highest economic effect and a balanced development of the economy, and the highest increment in output and national income per rouble spent. Emphasis must be shifted from new construction projects to technical re-equipment and reconstruction of existing enterprises, with a considerable increase in the share of funds spent on these purposes in the overall volume of productive capital investments, and with greater spending on equipment and machinery. The top-priority task is to improve the correlation between capital investments in resource-extracting, processing and consuming sectors and to redistribute funds in favour of the sectors which ensure the acceleration of scientific and technological progress.

Making the Soviet economy the most highly-developed and powerful one in the world calls for further development of **heavy industry** as the basis of economic strength.

The Party assigns to **machine-building** the key role in applying the latest achievements of science and technology. Higher growth rates in machine-building are the basis for scientific and technological progress in all sectors of the national economy and for maintaining the country's defences at a proper level, and represent the main trend in the long-range development of the economy. Machine-building is called upon to manufacture systems and sets of machinery, equipment and instruments of the highest technical and economic standards so as to ensure revolutionary changes in the technology and organisation of production, manifold increase in labour productivity, reduction in material intensity and power intensity, improvement in product quality, and higher returns on capital. Priority will be given to the development of machine-tool building, electrical engineering, the microelectronic industry, computer engineering and instrument-making, the entire branch of information science as the real catalysts for scientific and technological progress.

We must strengthen the potential of and effect a qualitative improvement in metallurgy, the chemical industry, and other sectors of heavy industry that produce **structural materials**, continuously broaden the range and improve the quality of materials, and increase the output of new, highly economical and advanced types.

The effective development of the **country's fuel-and-energy complex** is a most important task. Consistent satisfaction of the country's growing requirements for various types of fuel and energy requires improvement in the structure of the fuel-and-energy balance, accelerated development of the nuclear power industry, large-scale utilisation of renewable sources of energy, and vigorous and purposeful work to save fuel and energy resources in all sectors of the national economy.

An indispensable condition for social and economic progress is the further strengthening and improved efficiency of the **agro-industrial complex**, and a full satisfaction of the country's requirements in its produce. The task is to complete the transfer of agriculture to an industrial basis, introduce everywhere scientific systems of farming and intensive technologies, improve the utilisation of soil and raise its fertility, achieve a significant increase in the yield of agricultural crops and in livestock productivity, build up the fodder base, ensure stability in agricultural production, reduce its dependence on unfavourable natural and climatic conditions, and rule out losses in harvested farm crops and livestock produce. Agro-industrial integration and inter-farm cooperation will be consolidated; the machinery, technology and organisation of production, procurement, transportation, storage and processing of agricultural produce will be raised to a new level.

Collective and state farms, and agro-industrial associations and enterprises that form the backbone of socialist agriculture are called upon to contribute decisively to satisfying the country's requirements in agricultural produce. At the same time subsidiary farms run by enterprises and individual plots of citizens, as well as collective gardening, will be used to replenish the food resources.

The CPSU will direct efforts towards accelerated growth in the production of **consumer goods and the entire sphere of services** to satisfy completely the needs of the Soviet people. Enterprises, associations and organisations in all sectors of the national economy should be involved in this.

In perfecting the integral national economic complex of the country the Party assigns an important role to technical retooling and the more efficient performance of sectors of the **production infrastructure** – the systems of electric power, oil and gas supply, communications and information back-up. Special attention will be paid to developing an integrated transport system, upgrading all its

66

links, and developing a ramified network of well-appointed roads.

The task is essentially to raise technical and economic standards in **construction**, turn construction work into an integral industrial process, improve the quality and reduce the cost of design and construction work, and cut down the time taken to complete construction projects and to bring them up to design capacity.

The Party will continue to devote undivided attention to improving the **distribution of the productive forces**, an effort which should ensure the economy of social labour and the comprehensive and highly efficient development of each region. The economies of all Union republics will develop further through the greater social division of labour, and their contribution to the satisfaction of the requirements of the country will grow. The task is further to improve the structure of the existing territorial-production complexes and of economic ties, and to bring enterprises that process raw materials as close as possible to the places where those materials are extracted. It is necessary to use to a fuller extent the possibilities offered by small and medium-sized towns and workers' settlements, to locate within them specialised production facilities linked to the manufacture of products under co-production arrangements with major enterprises, to the processing of agricultural and local raw materials, and to the provision of services to the population.

Accelerated development of the productive forces in **Siberia and the Soviet Far East** remains a component part of the Party's economic strategy. In developing new regions it is of special economic and political importance strictly to ensure the comprehensive fulfilment of production tasks and the development of the entire social infrastructure so as to improve people's working and living conditions.

In charting economic development prospects, the CPSU proceeds from the need to improve **foreign economic strategy** and more fully to utilise the possibilities offered by the mutually advantageous international division of labour and, above all, the advantages of socialist economic integration. Foreign economic, scientific and technical contacts will be extended, and progressive structural changes will be introduced in the sphere of export and import in order to raise the efficiency of the national economy and guarantee independence from capitalist countries in strategically important areas.

Improvement of Socialist Production Relations, the System of Economic Management and Its Methods

Constant improvement of production relations, which should always correspond to the dynamically developing productive forces, and identification and resolution in good time of non-antagonistic contradictions arising between them are vital prerequisites for accelerating socio-economic progress.

Consolidation and enhancement of social ownership of the means of production, which is the foundation of the economic system of socialism, will remain at the centre of the Party's attention. The task is to increase the degree to which production is socialised, to raise the efficiency of its planned organisation, and steadily to improve the forms and methods of utilising the advantages and potentials of property belonging to all the people.

An upsurge of productive forces in agriculture, the development of inter-farm cooperation and agro-industrial integration will help bring about a further drawing together, and in the future a fusion, of collective-farm and cooperative property and the property of all the people. This will be a result of the all-round development and strengthening of both forms of socialist ownership, ever fuller utilisation of the possibilities of the collective-farm and cooperative sector of the economy.

The Party will persevere in fostering in work collectives and in every worker a sense of co-ownership of social property, take the necessary measures to protect socialist property, prevent all attempts to use it for self-serving ends, eradicate methods of appropriation of material benefits that are alien to socialism, and ensure the constitutional right of citizens to personal property.

The Party attaches great significance to **improvement of relations in the sphere of distribution** which have a notable effect on enhancing collective and personal interest in the development of social production and on the standards and mode of life of the people. A policy will be consistently implemented of ensuring the most effective distribution of the social product and national income, and making sure that the mechanism of distribution serves as a reliable barrier to unearned incomes and to levelling in pay, a barrier to everything that contradicts the norms and principles of socialist society. It is necessary to have strict control over the measure of work and the measure of consumption, to increase the interest of collectives and of every worker in achieving better national economic results, and skilfully to combine moral and material incentives in work.

An urgent task is further to develop **relations in the sphere of economic exchange**. It is necessary to increase the stability of economic ties, ensure a dynamic correlation between demand and supply, improve the circulation of material and money resources and accelerate the turnover of circulating assets.

To raise production efficiency and improve distribution, exchange and consumption it is important to use commodity-money relations more fully, in conformity with the new content inherent in them under socialism. It is necessary to promote greater economy and control over the amount and quality of work by using monetary means, to employ the whole arsenal of economic levers and incentives, to consolidate the state budget and to increase the buying power of the rouble.

The acceleration of the social and economic development of the country demands continuous **improvement in the guidance of the national economy**, reliable and effective functioning of the economic mechanism comprising diverse and flexible forms and methods of management, and their correspondence to changing conditions of economic development and the character of the tasks being fulfilled.

Improvement of management should be based on a more efficient and comprehensive use of the advantages and possibilities of the socialist planned economic system and economic laws, and take full account of the changes in productive forces and production relations and of the growth of educational standards, consciousness, qualifications and experience of the broad mass of the working people. It should ensure an optimal combination of personal interests and the interests of work collectives and of different social groups with the interests of the entire state, the interests of all the people, and in this way use them as the motive force of economic growth.

The entire system of management should be directed towards augmenting the contribution of every element of the national economy to attaining the supreme goal – to satisfy to the fullest extent the requirements of society. The all-round increase of this contribution with a minimum expenditure of all resources is an immutable law of socialist economic management, and the basic criterion for evaluating the performance of various sectors, associations and enterprises, of all production units.

There must be a consistent implementation of the Leninist principles of management and, above all, of the principle of **democratic centralism** which reflects the unity of both of its basic elements – enhanced efficiency of centralised guidance and a considerable broadening of the economic autonomy and responsibility of associations and enterprises.

The attention of central management bodies should be concentrated to an increasing degree on fulfilling the strategic tasks of economic and social development, and on implementing in practice a uniform policy in the spheres of scientific and technological progress and capital investments, of structural changes in the national economy, the proportionality of social production, the strengthening of the system of planned state reserves, distribution of the productive forces, payment for work, social security, prices, tariffs, finances, accounting and statistics.

The Party considers it necessary to raise the efficiency of **planning** as an instrument for carrying out its economic policy. Planning should be an active lever for accelerating the social and economic development of the country, for intensifying production on the basis of scientific and technological progress, implementing progressive economic decisions and ensuring balanced and dynamic economic growth. Qualitative indices reflecting the efficiency of utilisation of resources, the scale of output of new products and the growth of labour productivity on the basis of the achievements of science and technology should occupy a central place in plans. It is vital to tackle economic and social tasks comprehensively, organically combine long-term, five-year and annual plans, raise the scientific standards of planning, enhance discipline in carrying out plans, ensure priority of the interests of the entire state, and decisively put a stop to all manifestations of departmentalism and parochialism, red tape and voluntarism. The finance-and-credit system must be substantially improved, and its role in raising production efficiency and strengthening the money turnover system and cost accounting must be enhanced.

Developing the principles of centralised management and planning, the Party, in the fulfilment of strategic tasks, will vigorously carry out **measures to enhance the role of the main production element** – associations and enterprises, and consistently follow a line towards broadening their rights and economic autonomy and increasing their responsibility and interest in achieving good final results. Day-to-day management work should be concentrated at the local level – in work collectives.

The Party considers it necessary to develop and improve further the effectiveness of **cost accounting** and consistently to switch enterprises and associations over to full-scale cost accounting, while enhancing economic leverage and reducing the number of indices set by higher organisations. The activity of associations and enterprises will be regulated to an ever fuller extent by long-term economic norms which give scope to initiative and creativity in work collectives. Measures to improve management from above should be combined with the development of collective forms of organisation and stimulation of work at a grass-roots level. The system of levers and incentives should give real advantages to work collectives that are successful in accelerating scientific and technological progress, put out better products and increase the profitability of production. The opportunities and rights of associations and enterprises to use

70

money earned to develop production, provide material incentives for the work force and resolve social questions will grow.

Wholesale trade will expand, the role of direct ties and economic contracts between the consumer-enterprises and manufacturers of products will grow, and so will the influence of the consumer on the technical standards and quality of products.

Price-formation must be improved to ensure that prices reflect more accurately the level of socially indispensable inputs and the quality of products and services, that they stimulate more actively scientific and technological progress, thrift in the use of resources, improvement of technical, economic and consumer qualities of products and introduction of all things new and advanced, and that they promote greater economy.

The CPSU sets the task of consistently improving the **organisational structure of the management** of the national economy at all levels, reducing the managerial apparatus and doing away with its excessive elements. It is necessary to improve the management of major national economic complexes and groups of interrelated and similar sectors; to achieve a rational combination of large, medium-sized and small enterprises, and of sectoral and territorial management; to extend the network and improve the performance of production and research-and-production associations; to deepen specialisation; and to develop integration and cooperation in production.

The attention of inter-sectoral and sectoral management bodies will be concentrated on the most important trends in the development of various sectors and on the introduction of scientific and technological achievements. They should be responsible for meeting fully the requirements of the national economy and the population for products of the range and variety that have been decided on. The role and responsibility of republican and local bodies in managing economic, social and cultural development and in meeting the needs of the working people will grow, and the powers of these bodies will be broadened.

In its work to improve economic guidance the CPSU will consistently pursue a line towards **developing the working people's creative initiative and their increased involvement in the process of managing production**, a line towards enhancing the role of work collectives in drafting plans and making economic decisions, in implementing measures in the field of social and economic development at enterprises, and in finding and mobilising the internal reserves of production. Thriftiness, the efficient use of public funds, rational use of every rouble, eradication of mismanagement, and elimination of various non-productive expenditures and losses – this

71

is the cause of the entire Party, all the people, every work collective, every worker.

The development of **socialist emulation** is a subject to which the Party gives constant attention. It is one of the most important spheres for encouraging the creativity of working people, one of the chief means of self-expression and social recognition of the individual. Guided by the Leninist principles of openness and the possibility to compare results and to draw on advanced experience, we must improve the organisation and enhance the efficiency of emulation, root out formalism and stereotypes, and develop the spirit of initiative, comradely cooperation and mutual assistance. Of great significance is all-round support for the initiative and creativity of the people in accelerating scientific and technological progress, increasing labour productivity, ensuring the thrifty use of resources, improving production efficiency and output quality while reducing output costs, ensuring an efficient work rhythm with timely fulfil-ment of contractual obligations and achieving better national economic results.

III. The Social Policy of the Party

The Party regards social policy as a powerful means of accelerating the country's development, heightening the labour and socio-political activity of the masses, moulding the new man, and affirming the socialist way of life, and as a major factor of political stability in society. It proceeds from the belief that the influence of social policy on growing economic efficiency – on all aspects of public life – will intensify. The CPSU considers undiminishing concern for solving the social questions of labour, everyday needs and culture, for meeting the interests and requirements of the people to be the supreme aim of the activity of all state and economic bodies and public organisa-tions.

The Party defines the principal tasks of social policy as follows:

– a steady improvement of the living and working conditions of Soviet people;
– the implementation to an ever fuller extent of the principle of social justice in all spheres of social relations;
– a drawing closer together of all classes and social groups and strata, overcoming essential distinctions between mental and physical work, between town and countryside;
– the perfection of relations between nations and ethnic groups; strengthening the fraternal friendship of the peoples and nationalities of the country.

*Raising the Well-Being and Improving the Living and Working
Conditions of Soviet People*

The production and intellectual potential created in the Soviet Union,
and the tasks of accelerating the country's social and economic
development make it necessary and possible to achieve notable
progress in attaining 'full well-being and free, **all-round** development for **all** the members of society' (Lenin).

The CPSU sets the task of improving the well-being of Soviet
people so as to give it a qualitatively new dimension, of ensuring
that the level and structure of consumption of material, social and
cultural benefits will correspond most fully to the aim of moulding
a harmoniously developed, spiritually rich individual and creating the
necessary conditions for the full application of the abilities and
talents of Soviet people in the interests of society.

Already in the next fifteen years it is planned to double the volume
of resources channelled into meeting the requirements of the people.

**The Party attaches special importance to enhancing the
creative content and collectivist character of work, improving its
efficiency, and encouraging highly skilled and highly productive
labour for the good of society.** All this will help make work a
prime vital necessity for every Soviet person.

The task ahead is to continue to carry out a series of scientific,
technological, economic and social measures aimed at ensuring full
and effective employment of the population, and granting to all able-
bodied citizens the possibility to work in their chosen sphere of
activity in accordance with their inclinations, abilities, education and
training, with due account of the needs of society.

A consistent policy will be carried out to decrease considerably the
amount of manual work, reduce substantially, and in the future
eliminate altogether, monotonous, arduous physical and low-skilled
work, ensure healthy, hygienic conditions and introduce better
production safety norms in order to prevent industrial accidents and
occupational diseases. Intensification and increased efficiency of
production and labour productivity will open up in the future new
possibilities for reducing working hours and extending the period of
paid holidays.

**The Party will continue to do everything necessary to raise
steadily the real incomes of working people and further to
improve the well-being of all strata and social groups in accordance with the country's economic possibilities.**

Payment according to work done remains the principal source of
working people's incomes during the first phase of communism. The
system of wages and salaries must be improved constantly so that it

fully corresponds to the principle of payment according to the amount and quality of work done, with due account of the conditions and results of work, stimulates the upgrading of workers' skills and labour productivity, and promotes better output quality and the rational use and saving of all types of resources. It is on this basis that the wages and salaries of working people should grow and their living standards improve. As social wealth grows, the size of minimum wages will increase and the policy of reducing personal income taxes will be carried on. The Party attaches fundamental significance to the resolute elimination of unearned incomes, the eradication of all deviations from the socialist principles of distribution.

Accelerated growth and improvement of the distribution of **social consumption funds** will continue. These funds are to play an increasing role in the development of the state system of free public education and free public health service and social security, in improving the conditions of rest and recreation for working people, in lessening the differences that are objectively inevitable under socialism in the material status of citizens, families and social groups, in evening out socio-economic and cultural conditions for the upbringing of children and in helping to improve radically the well-being of low-income groups of the population.

A task of foremost importance is **to meet completely the growing demand of the population for high-quality and diverse consumer goods** – foodstuffs, durable and beautiful clothing and footwear, furniture, commodities for cultural needs, and sophisticated household appliances and goods.

Domestic retail trade and public catering will be further developed. Their material and technical basis will be improved and the standards of service will be raised. Consumers' cooperatives, which are to improve trade in the countryside, organise the purchase of farm produce grown by the population and the marketing of agricultural products, will also be further developed. The collective-farm market will continue to play a significant role. A policy of retail prices will be pursued in the interests of increasing people's real incomes.

It is planned to carry out large-scale measures for the setting up of a **modern, highly developed service sector**. An increase in the volume of services, a broadening of their range and improvement of their quality will make it possible to meet more fully the growing demand of the population for various types of communal, transport, everyday, social and cultural services, to make housework easier, and to create better conditions for rest and a meaningful use of free time. The service industry will expand at an accelerated rate in the countryside and in the regions now being developed.

The Party considers as a matter of special social significance an accelerated solution of the **housing problem**, which will ensure that by the year 2000 practically every Soviet family will have their own living quarters – an apartment or an individual house. This end will be served by the large scale of state-funded housing construction, more extensive development of cooperative and individual house building, as well as reconstruction, renovation and better upkeep of the available housing and stricter control over its distribution. Special attention will be devoted to the quality of housing construction, to improving the standards of comfort, layouts and technical equipment of apartments and houses.

Higher demands will be made on the architecture, landscaping and planning of urban and rural settlements. Such population centres should be a well thought-out arrangement of production zones, residential districts, public, cultural, educational and child-care institutions, trade and service establishments, sports facilities, and public transport, ensuring the best conditions for work, everyday life and rest. The practice of encouraging people to contribute funds for the improvement of living conditions, cultural and recreation facilities, tourism and other activities will be broadened.

A matter of primary importance is **building up the health of Soviet people** and prolonging the period of their active life. The Party sets the task of satisfying completely the requirements of urban and rural residents everywhere for all types of medical services of a high standard, and of radically improving the quality of medical services. To this end it is planned: to introduce a universal system of medical check-ups for the population; to extend further the network of mother-and-child-care centres, clinics, hospitals and sanatoria and to equip them with modern medical facilities; and to ensure the necessary supply of medicines, medical equipment and sanitation and hygiene means.

Physical training and sports are a factor of everyday life. Their importance is growing in improving people's health, in the harmonious development of the individual and in preparing youth for work and the defence of their homeland. Efforts should be made to ensure that every person cares for his physical fitness from an early age, has a knowledge of hygiene and medical aid and has a healthy way of life.

The CPSU attaches great significance to **showing more care for the family**. The family plays an important role in building up the health of the younger generation and in its upbringing, in ensuring the economic and social progress of society and in improving demographic processes. It is in the family that one's basic character, one's attitude to work and to moral, ideological and cultural values take shape. Society is vitally interested in having families that are stable and spiritually and morally healthy. Proceeding from this, the Party considers it necessary to pursue a policy of strengthening the family and rendering assistance to it in the performance of its social functions and in the upbringing of children, a policy of improving the material, housing and living conditions of families with children and of newly married couples. There must be a more profound cooperation between the family, the school and the work collective; it is necessary to enhance the responsibility of parents for the upbringing of children, as well as the responsibility of children for the well-being of parents, for their secure old age.

A matter of continuing concern to the Party is a **further improvement of the status of mothers**. To this end favourable conditions will be created that will enable women to combine motherhood with active participation in work and social activities. Special attention will be devoted to mother-and-child care, and the period of pre-natal and child-care leave will be extended. The network of sanatoria, rest homes and boarding houses that accommodate families on holiday will be expanded. Diverse forms of employing women will be further developed. Sliding work schedules, a shorter working day, and work at home will be introduced on a wider scale in accordance with the wishes of women.

A broad range of measures will be implemented to create the necessary conditions for the upbringing of the younger generation. In the near future the demand of the population for child-care establishments will be met in full. The network of Young Pioneer and work-and-sports camps, Young Pioneer houses, and scientific and technical and creative art centres and stations will be expanded. The norms of expenditures on catering in pre-school and vocational training establishments and in children's homes will grow.

The Party stresses the need to give considerably **more attention to the social problems of young people** and, above all, to develop and more fully satisfy those interests and requirements of young people that are socially significant, in the sphere of work and everyday life, education and culture, professional advancement and promotion, and rational use of free time.

The CPSU will continue to show constant **concern for improving the material status of labour and war veterans**, senior citizens, disabled persons, and the families of soldiers killed on duty, for providing social, medical and cultural services to them. The sizes of pensions and, above all, minimum pensions and those granted earlier will be periodically increased. The level of pensions provided to collective farmers will gradually approach that established for production and office workers. The network of homes for the aged and disabled will be further developed and the conditions of upkeep in such homes will be improved. Labour veterans with valuable experience will have more opportunities to work in accordance with their capabilities and to be involved in public life and educational work; this is a matter of major social and economic importance.

The harmonious interaction between society and nature, between man and the environment is acquiring ever growing significance in improving the life of the people. Socialist society, which consciously builds its future, manages the use of nature in a planned and thrifty manner and is in the vanguard of mankind's struggle to preserve and augment the natural wealth of our planet. The Party considers it necessary to exercise greater control over nature management and to conduct ecological education on a wider scale.

Overcoming Class Differences and the Formation of a Socially Homogeneous Society

An important law of the development of social relations at the present stage is the **drawing closer together of the working class, the collective-farm peasantry and the intelligentsia, and the establishment of a classless structure of society with the working class playing the decisive role in that process.**

The political experience of the working class, its high level of consciousness, organisation and will provide a rallying point for our society. The growth of the general educational and cultural standards and skills, and of the labour and socio-political activity of the working class enhances its vanguard role in perfecting socialism, in building communism.

In the course of consistently implementing the Party's agrarian policy, agricultural work is turned into a variety of industrial work and the substantial social differences and differences in cultural and service standards between town and country are being eliminated. The way of life and the character of work of the peasants are becoming increasingly similar to those of the working class. Overcoming the differences between these classes and establishing a classless society in our country will take place mainly in the historical framework of the first, socialist phase of the communist formation.

Revolutionary transformations of the productive forces are leading to an increase in the share of brain work in the activities of the broad mass of workers and collective-farm peasants. At the same time, the numerical strength of the intelligentsia is growing and its creative contribution to material production and other spheres of public life is increasing. This promotes a gradual elimination of the

77

substantial differences between physical and brain work and the drawing closer together of all social groups. The complete elimination of these differences and the formation of a socially homogeneous society will take place at the supreme phase of communism. At the same time, as long as such differences exist, the Party considers it a matter of foremost importance to take careful account in its policies of the distinctive features characterising the interests of the classes and social groups. Much attention will be given to evening out the working and living conditions of the population in different regions of the country.

The role of work collectives in the social structure of Soviet society **is growing**. The Party is helping in every way to bring about a situation in which every work collective will become an effective social cell of socialist self-government by the people and day-to-day genuine participation of working people in the solution of questions related to the work of enterprises, institutions and organisations, and of the development and application of the creative energies of the individual. It considers it necessary to enhance in a purposeful manner the influence of work collectives on all spheres of the life of society, to extend their rights and at the same time to increase their responsibility for carrying out specific tasks of economic, social and cultural development.

Further Flourishing and Drawing Closer Together of Socialist Nations and Nationalities

The CPSU takes full account in its activities of the multinational composition of Soviet society. The path that has been traversed provides convincing proof that **the nationalities question inherited from the past has been successfully solved in the Soviet Union**. Characteristic of the national relations in our country are both the continued flourishing of the nations and nationalities and the fact that they are steadily and voluntarily drawing closer together on the basis of equality and fraternal cooperation. Neither artificial prodding nor holding back of the objective trends of development is admissible here. In the long-term historical perspective this development will lead to complete unity of the nations.

The CPSU proceeds from the fact that in our socialist multinational state, in which more than one hundred nations and nationalities work and live together, there naturally arise **new tasks of improving national relations**. The Party has carried out, and will continue to carry out such tasks on the basis of the tested principles of the Leninist nationalities policy. It puts forward the following main tasks in this field:

– all-round strengthening and development of the integral, federal, multinational state. The CPSU will continue to struggle consistently against any manifestations of parochialism and national narrow-mindedness, while at the same time showing constant concern for further increasing the role of the republics, autonomous regions and autonomous areas in carrying out countrywide tasks and for promoting the active involvement of working people of all nationalities in the work of government and administrative bodies. Through creative application of the Leninist principles of socialist federalism and democratic centralism, the forms of inter-nation relations will be enriched in the interests of the Soviet people as a whole and of each nation and nationality;

– a buildup of the material and intellectual potential of each republic within the framework of the integral national economic complex. Combining the initiative of the Union and autonomous republics, autonomous regions and autonomous areas with central administration at the countrywide level will make possible the more rational use of the country's resources and of local natural and other features. It is necessary consistently to deepen the division of labour between the republics, even out the conditions of economic management, encourage active participation by the republics in the economic development of new regions, promote inter-republican exchanges of workers and specialists, and broaden and improve the training of qualified personnel from among citizens of all the nations and nationalities inhabiting the republics;

– development of the Soviet people's integral culture which is socialist in content, diverse in its national forms and internationalist in spirit, on the basis of the greatest achievements and original progressive traditions of the peoples of the USSR. The advancement and drawing together of the national cultures and the consolidation of their interrelationships make mutual enrichment more fruitful and open up the broadest possibilities for the Soviet people to enjoy everything valuable that has been created by the talent of each of the peoples of our country.

The equal right of all citizens of the USSR to use their native languages and the free development of these languages will be ensured in the future as well. At the same time learning the Russian language, which has been voluntarily accepted by the Soviet people as a medium of communication between different nationalities, besides the language of one's nationality, broadens one's access to the achievements of science and technology and of Soviet and world culture.

The Party proceeds from the belief that consistent implementation

of the Leninist nationalities policy and a strengthening in every way
of the friendship of the peoples are part of the effort to perfect
socialism and a way that has been tested in social practice of ensuring the further flourishing of our multinational socialist homeland.

IV. Development of the Political System of Soviet Society

Established as a result of the socialist revolution, the dictatorship of
the proletariat played the decisive role in creating the new society,
and in the process it, too, underwent changes. With the abolition of
the exploiter classes the function of suppressing the resistance of the
overthrown exploiters gradually faded away and full scope was given
to accomplishing its foremost, constructive tasks. Having fulfilled its
historical mission, the dictatorship of the proletariat has evolved into
a political power of all working people, while the proletarian state
has become a state of the whole people. It is the main tool for
perfecting socialism in our country, while on the international scene
it performs the functions of upholding the socialist gains, strengthening the positions of world socialism, countering the aggressive policy
of imperialist forces and developing peaceful cooperation with all
nations.

**The CPSU believes that at the present stage the strategic line
of development of the political system of Soviet society consists in
advancing Soviet democracy and increasingly promoting socialist
self-government by the people on the basis of active and effective
participation of working people, their collectives and organisations in decision-making concerning the affairs of state and
society.**

The leading force in this process is the Party, the nucleus of the
political system of Soviet society. It exercises guidance over the
work of all other parts of this system – the Soviet state, the trade
unions, the Young Communist League, the cooperatives and other
public organisations reflecting the common and specific interests of
all sections of the population, of all the nations and nationalities of
the country. Acting within the framework of the Constitution, the
CPSU directs and coordinates the work of state and public organisations and sees to it that each of them fully carries out its functions.
In all its activities the Party sets an example of serving the interests
of the people and observing the principles of socialist democracy.

The Party makes sure that the principles of socialist self-
government by the people are consistently applied in the administration of society and the state, that is, that the work of administration
is not only carried out in the interests of working people but also
becomes naturally, and to an ever greater extent, a direct concern of

working people themselves, who, to use Lenin's words, know no authority except the authority of their own unity.

The Party will continue to work to ensure that the socio-economic, political and personal rights and freedoms of citizens are extended and enriched and that ever more favourable conditions and guarantees are created for their full exercise. Soviet citizens have every possibility to express and exercise their civic will and interests and enjoy all the benefits of socialism. Soviet citizens' exercise of their rights and freedoms is inseparable from the performance of their constitutional duties. It is an immutable political principle of socialist society that there are no rights without duties and no duties without rights. The CPSU will continue its persistent efforts to make sure that every Soviet citizen is educated in a spirit of awareness of the indivisibility of his rights, freedoms and duties.

It is a matter of key importance for the Party's policy to **develop and strengthen the Soviet socialist state** and increasingly reveal its democratic nature as a state of the whole people and its creative and constructive role.

The CPSU makes constant efforts to improve the work of the Soviets of People's Deputies – the political foundation of the USSR, the main element in socialist self-government by the people. The Party attaches great significance to perfecting the forms of the people's representation, to developing the democratic principles of the Soviet electoral system and to ensuring free, comprehensive discussion of the candidates' personal and professional qualities so that the most capable and respected representatives of the working class, collective-farm peasantry and the people's intelligentsia of all the nations and nationalities of the country are elected to the Soviets. In order to improve the work of the Soviets and infuse fresh blood into them, in order that more millions of people will go through the school of running the state, the composition of deputies to the Soviets will be systematically renewed at elections.

The CPSU makes a constant effort to facilitate the work of the Supreme Soviet of the USSR and the Supreme Soviets of the Union republics of consistently perfecting legislation, effectively resolving the key problems of home and foreign policy within their sphere of responsibilities, exercising vigorous guidance over the Soviets of People's Deputies and checking on the work done by the agencies under them. The role and responsibility of local Soviets in ensuring the comprehensive economic and social development of their respective regions, in implementing tasks of local significance and in coordinating and checking on the activities of organisations in their areas will continue to grow.

All conditions should be created for the strict fulfilment of Lenin's instructions that the Soviets should be bodies that not only make decisions but also organise and check on their implementation. Soviets at all levels should apply ever more fully democratic principles of work, including collective, free and constructive discussion and decision-making; publicity; criticism and self-criticism; the deputies' regular reporting back to the constituencies and their accountability to them to the extent of being recalled before the expiration of their term of office for having failed to justify the voters' confidence; control over the work done by executive and other bodies; and extensive involvement of citizens in the work of administration.

The Party will unswervingly conduct a policy of **democratising administration, the process of working out and adopting decisions of state importance**, which ensures selection of optimal solutions and the consideration and comparison of different opinions and proposals put forward by the working people. The range of matters to be decided on only after discussion in work collectives, standing commissions of the Soviets, and trade union, YCL and other public organisations will broaden. The more important draft laws and decisions will be submitted for countrywide discussion and put to a popular vote. The task is to continue to improve the system of summing up and fulfilling mandates given by electors to their candidates in elections and other suggestions and proposals from citizens and of studying public opinion, and to enable the people to be better informed about the decisions taken and the results of their implementation.

Of particular importance is the broadening of the rights and a heightening of the activity of work collectives in all matters of managing production, social and cultural development and in the political life of society. Steps will be taken to enhance the role of general meetings and councils of work collectives and the responsibility of the management for the fulfilment of their decisions, and to introduce the election of foremen, heads of sections and leaders of other production units.

It is a matter of great importance to improve the performance of the state apparatus and all other administrative bodies. The Soviet apparatus serves the people and is accountable to the people. It should be highly competent and efficient. It is necessary to work for a streamlining of the administrative machinery, a reduction of costs and elimination of redundant jobs, persistently to eradicate manifestations of red tape, formalism, departmentalism and parochialism and get rid of incompetent and inert officials without delay. Careless work, abuse of office, careerism, striving for personal enrichment, nepotism and favouritism should be relentlessly rooted out and punished.

The Party considers it necessary to abide strictly by the principle of accountability of the staff of state bodies and extend the system of filling vacancies through election or competition. It is necessary persistently to implement the principle of collective decision-making, with each executive remaining personally responsible for the work done; members of the staff should be judged objectively by their practical work and there should be effective control over the actual fulfilment of the decisions taken.

The CPSU will actively help to raise the efficiency of state and public control. It regards the participation of working people in **People's Control** bodies as an important way of increasing their political maturity and heightening their activity in protecting public interests, and of fostering a statesmanlike approach to matters and a caring attitude to public property.

It has been and remains a matter of unremitting concern to the Party to **strengthen the legal foundation of the life of the state and society**, ensure strict observance of socialist law and order, and improve the work of judicial bodies, the work of supervision by agencies of the Procurator's Office, and the work of justice and internal affairs bodies. Relying on the support of work collectives, public organisation and all working people, state bodies are obliged to do everything necessary to ensure the safety and good condition of socialist property, protect the personal property of citizens, their honour and dignity, wage an unrelenting struggle against crime, drunkenness and alcoholism, prevent offences of any kind and remove their causes.

The Communist Party of the Soviet Union regards defence of the socialist homeland, a strengthening of the country's defences and the ensuring of state security as one of the most important functions of the Soviet state.

From the standpoint of the country's internal conditions our society does not need an army. But as long as there exists the danger of imperialism starting aggressive wars and military conflicts, the Party will be paying unflagging attention to enhancing the defence capacity of the USSR, strengthening its security and ensuring the preparedness of its Armed Forces to rout any aggressor. The Armed Forces and the state security bodies should display high vigilance and be always ready to cut short imperialism's intrigues against the USSR and its allies.

The leadership exercised by the Communist Party over the country's military development and the Armed Forces is the basis for strengthening the defences of the socialist homeland. It is under the Party's guidance that the country's policy in the field of defence and security and the Soviet military doctrine, which is purely defensive in nature and geared to ensuring protection against an outside attack, are worked out and implemented.

The CPSU will make every effort to ensure that the Soviet Armed Forces remain at a level that rules out strategic superiority of the forces of imperialism, that the Soviet state's defence capacity continues to be improved in every way and that military cooperation between the armies of the fraternal socialist countries is strengthened.

The Party will continue to make constant efforts to ensure that the combat potential of the Soviet Armed Forces is a firm union of military skill, a high level of technical capability, ideological staunchness, organisation and discipline of the officers and men and their loyalty to their patriotic and internationalist duty.

The CPSU considers it necessary in the future as well to increase its organising and directing influence on the Armed Forces' activities, strengthen the principle of one-man leadership, broaden the role and influence of the political bodies and Party organisation of the Army and the Navy and make sure that the Armed Forces' vital links with the people will become still stronger. It is the duty of every Communist, every Soviet citizen to do everything possible to maintain the country's defence capacity at an adequate level. **Defence of the socialist homeland and military service in the ranks of the Armed Forces are an honourable and sacred duty of Soviet citizens.**

The Party attaches foremost importance to enhancing the role of public organisations, which are important component parts of the system of socialist self-government by the people.

The CPSU regards it as its task to promote the continued growth of the prestige and influence of the **trade unions**, which are the most broadly-based organisation of the working people, a school of administration, a school of economic management and a school of communism. The trade unions are to discharge their main functions consistently: to do everything possible to help increase public wealth, improve the working people's working and everyday-life conditions and recreation facilities, protect their rights and interests, be constantly involved in the communist education of the people and draw them into the management of production and the affairs of society, and strengthen conscious labour discipline.

It is the task of trade-union organisations to take an even more active part in promoting socialist self-government by the people and in solving the fundamental questions of the development of the state, economy and culture, interact more closely with the Soviets and other organisations of the working people, raise the standards of the socialist emulation movement and of the effort to disseminate advanced experience and promote its wider application, develop social forms of control over the observance of the principles of social justice and help work collectives exercise the powers vested in them.

The CPSU justly regards as its active helpmate and dependable reserve the **All-Union Leninist Young Communist League**, a public political organisation whose membership of many millions represents the advanced section of Soviet youth. The Party will continue to increase the YCL's role in the education of the younger generation, in the improvement of the work of the Young Pioneer organisation, and in the practical implementation of the tasks of speeding up the country's social and economic development. Exercising guidance over the YCL, the CPSU pays special attention to strengthening its ranks organisationally and politically and enhancing the independent character of the youth league The YCL should persistently promote the labour and social activity of young people, instill in them a Marxist-Leninist world outlook and high political and moral standards and help them become aware of their historical responsibility for the future of socialism and the world.

The Party helps to improve the work of the **cooperatives** – collective farms, consumer and home-building cooperatives and other cooperative organisations and associations, regarding them as an important form of socialist self-government and an effective means of developing the national economy.

The CPSU will facilitate a further heightening of the activity of the **unions of workers in the arts, of scientific, science and technology, cultural and educational, sport, defence and other voluntary societies and people's social activity bodies**. In fulfilling their functions, these organisations are to make an ever greater contribution to furthering the Party's policy and work for the all-round expression and satisfaction of the interests of the working people united in them, and for enhancing the Soviet people's civic initiative and sense of responsibility.

V. Ideological and Educational Work, Public Education, Science and Culture

The Party will do everything necessary for using in full measure the transforming force of Marxist-Leninist ideology to accelerate the country's social and economic development, and will conduct purposeful work for the ideological, political, labour and moral education of the Soviet people and for **moulding harmoniously developed, socially active individuals combining cultural wealth, moral purity and a perfect physique.**

The CPSU regards it as the main tasks of its ideological work to educate the working people in a spirit of high ideological integrity and dedication to communism, Soviet patriotism and proletarian, socialist internationalism, and a conscientious attitude towards work and public property, to make cultural and intellectual treasures ever more readily available to the people and to eradicate the morals that contradict the socialist way of life.

The Party proceeds from the conviction that a person's education is inseparable from his practical involvement in constructive work for the benefit of the people, in public life and in solving the tasks of social, economic, and cultural advancement. Detachment from reality and its problems dooms ideological and educational work to abstract instruction and empty rhetoric, leading it away from the pressing tasks of building communism. Ideological work should be characterised by close links with social practice, profound ideological and theoretical content and taking account fully and accurately of the realities of domestic and international life and of the growing intellectual requirements of the working people; it should be close to the people, truthful, well argued and comprehensible.

Unity of word and deed − the most important principle of all Party and state activities − is also an indispensable requirement of political and educational work. Active participation in this work is a duty of all leading cadres, a duty of every Communist.

The Party puts forward the following tasks:

In the Field of Ideological and Educational Work

The shaping of a scientific world outlook. Socialism has given Soviet society's intellectual and cultural life a scientific world outlook based on Marxism-Leninism, which is an integral and harmonious system of philosophical, economic and socio-political views. The Party considers it its most important duty to continue creatively developing Marxist-Leninist theory by studying and generalising new phenomena in Soviet society, taking into account the experience of other countries of the socialist community and the world communist, working-class, national liberation and democratic movements and analysing the progress in the natural, technical and social sciences.

The CPSU will work unremittingly so that all Soviet people can thoroughly study the Marxist-Leninist theory, raise their political awareness, consciously participate in the shaping of the Party's policy and actively implement it.

Labour education. In educational work the Party focuses its attention on instilling in all Soviet citizens deep respect and readiness for conscientious work for the common good, be it mental or physical work. Labour is the main source of society's material and cultural wealth, the principal criterion of a person's social status, his sacred duty and the cornerstone of his communist education. The Party will make continued efforts to increase the prestige of honest, efficient work, encourage labour initiative and innovation and strengthen the principles of the communist attitude towards work.

The affirmation of communist morality. In the gradual advancement towards communism the creative potential of communist morality, the most humane, just and noble morality, based on devotion to the goals of the revolutionary struggle and the ideals of communism, manifests itself ever more fully. Our morality has assimilated both universal moral values and the norms of conduct and norms governing relations between people, which have been established by the popular masses in the course of their centuries-old struggle against exploitation, for freedom and social equality, for happiness and peace.

The communist morality upheld by the CPSU is as follows:

– **a collectivist morality**, the fundamental principle of which is 'One for all and all for one'. This morality is incompatible with egoism and selfishness; it harmoniously blends the common, collective and personal interests of the people;

– **a humanistic morality**, which ennobles the working man, is filled with a deep respect for him and is intolerant of infringements upon his dignity. It asserts truly humane relations between people – relations of comradely cooperation and mutual assistance, good will, honesty, simplicity and modesty in private and public life;

– **an active, vigorous morality**, which stimulates one to ever new labour achievements and creative accomplishments, and encourages one to take a personal interest and be involved in the affairs of one's work collective and of the entire country, to be implacable in rejecting everything that contradicts the socialist way of life and to be persistent in the struggle for the communist ideals.

Patriotic and internationalist education. The Party will continue to work tirelessly so that in every Soviet citizen feelings of love for the country of the October Revolution where he was born and grew up, and pride for the historic accomplishments of the world's first socialist state are combined with feelings of loyalty to proletarian, socialist internationalism, of class solidarity with the working people of the fraternal countries, with all who are fighting against imperialism, and for social progress and peace.

The CPSU and the Soviet state want to see feelings of friendship and fraternity uniting all nations and nationalities of the USSR, a high standard of relations between nationalities and intolerance of any manifestations of nationalism, chauvinism, national narrow-mindedness or egoism, as well as attitudes and traditions that hinder the communist renovation of life become part of every Soviet citizen.

An important task of the Party in its ideological and educational work continues to be that of providing military-patriotic education and ensuring that everyone is prepared to defend the socialist homeland, to give it all his energies and, if necessary, to sacrifice his life for it.

Legal education. The Party attaches great importance to instilling in people a high sense of civic responsibility, respect for Soviet laws and the rules of socialist conduct, irreconcilability to any violations of socialist legality, and a readiness to take an active part in the maintenance of law and order.

Atheistic education. The Party uses ideological means for the broad dissemination of a scientific materialist world outlook, and for overcoming religious prejudices, while at the same time respecting the feelings of believers. While calling for the strict observance of the constitutional guarantees of freedom of conscience, the Party condemns attempts to use religion to the detriment of society and the individual. A highly important aspect of atheistic education consists in heightening the people's labour and public activity, raising their educational level, and the broad dissemination of new Soviet traditions and customs.

The struggle against manifestations of alien ideology and morals and all negative phenomena, connected with the vestiges of the past in the minds and behaviour of people as well as with short-comings in the practical work in various fields of public life, with delays in solving urgent problems, is an integral part of communist education. The Party attaches paramount importance to the steady and consistent eradication of violations of labour discipline, embezzlement and bribery, profiteering and parasitism, drunkenness and hooliganism, private-owner psychology and money-grubbing, toadyism and servility. It is essential to make full use of both the power of public opinion and the force of law for combating these phenomena.

Struggle against bourgeois ideology. The acute struggle between the two world outlooks on the international scene reflects the opposition of the two world systems – socialism and capitalism. The CPSU regards it as its task to tell people the truth about real socialism, about the domestic and foreign policy of the Soviet Union, actively to advocate the Soviet way of life and vigorously to expose in a well-argued manner the anti-popular, inhuman and exploitative nature of imperialism. It will instill in Soviet people a high level of political awareness, vigilance, and the ability to assess social phenomena and uphold the ideals and spiritual values of socialism from clear-cut class positions.

The mass information and propaganda media play a growing role in the life of society. The CPSU will make every effort to ensure that the media analyse trends and phenomena in domestic and international life as well as economic and social phenomena in depth, that they actively support everything new and advanced, and call attention to pressing issues of concern to the people and suggest ways of solving them. The press, television and radio networks should provide people with news coverage and commentary that are politically clear and purposeful, profound, prompt, informative, vivid and comprehensible. The Party will continue to render the press and all other mass media ready assistance and support in their work.

Special attention will be devoted to developing television broadcasting, ensuring that radio and TV programmes are increasingly available to the population, making the broadcasts richer in content and more interesting and raising their ideological and artistical level.

It is essential to resolutely eliminate any manifestations of pompous verbosity and formalism in ideological, educational, and propaganda work. All forms and means of this work must help mobilise the people for fulfilling the tasks facing the country by ensuring broad publicity of the work of the Party and state bodies and public organisations, direct and frank discussion with people, and by shaping public opinion and promoting its influence on practical matters. The CPSU will take constant care of strengthening the material foundation of ideological work.

In the Field of Public Education

The Party consistently pursues a policy of educating and training conscientious, highly-educated people fitted for both physical and mental work, for energetically accomplishing their jobs in the national economy, in various fields of public and state life, in science and in culture. The genuinely popular system of education established in the USSR has brought knowledge within the reach of all citizens and made it possible within a historically short span of time to eliminate widespread illiteracy and introduce universal secondary education.

The CPSU will continue improving the public education system, taking into account the need to accelerate social and

economic development, the prospects of communist construction and the requirements of scientific and technological progress. The reform of the general education and vocational training school now being effected in the country is based on the creative development of Lenin's principles of a uniform polytechnical labour school; it is aimed at raising still higher the standards of instruction and education of the young, and making them better prepared for their future labour activity, and geared toward gradually introducing universal vocational training. Schools are called upon to instill in their pupils love for their homeland, collectivism and respect for the elderly, for their parents and teachers, to impart to the younger generation a keen sense of responsibility for the quality of their study and work and for their conduct, and also to encourage student self-administration. As the planned measures are carried out, the vocational training and general education forms of schooling will continue to develop and draw closer together, with their eventual merging.

In keeping with the demands of scientific, technological and social progress, the system of secondary specialised and higher education will be further developed. It should respond readily and timely to the requirements of production, science and culture and meet the national economy's needs for specialists with high professional standards, ideological and political maturity and organisational and managerial skills. The Party attaches much significance to developing the system of advanced training which, combined with the system of correspondence and evening courses, will offer favourable opportunities for all working people to continue their education, steadily increase and refresh their knowledge and raise their general cultural and professional levels.

The Party will show unfailing concern for the teaching staff and for strengthening and extending the material foundation of the entire system of education.

In the Field of Science

Science is playing a growing role in developing the productive forces, perfecting social relations, creating fundamentally new kinds of equipment and technology, raising labour productivity, developing natural resources in the depths of the earth and the ocean, exploring outer space and protecting and improving the environment.

The Party's policy in the field of science is designed to create favourable conditions for dynamic progress in all areas of knowledge; concentrate personnel, and material and financial resources in the more promising areas of research called upon to

accelerate the accomplishment of planned economic and social tasks and society's cultural advancement; and ensure a reliable defence capability of the country.

Dialectical materialistic methods have been and remain the chief, tried-and-tested basis for progress in the natural sciences and social studies. They should be creatively further developed and skilfully applied in research and in social practice.

Soviet science is called upon to take leading positions in the principal areas of scientific and technological progress and to provide effective and timely solutions to current and long-term production, social and economic problems. It is important to ensure priority development of fundamental, exploratory research and ensure prompt implementation of scientific ideas in the national economy and other fields of endeavour. The organisational and economic forms of the integration of science and production and of directing scientific and technological progress should be continuously updated; the scale of topical applied research and experimental design projects and their efficiency should be increased. It is essential to strengthen the interaction of scientific work collectives at research institutions, higher educational establishments and in production.

Social science workers should focus their attention on studying and thoroughly analysing the experience of world development and the building of the new society in the USSR and other socialist countries, the dialectics of productive forces and relations of production and of the material and cultural spheres under socialism, the general laws governing the formation of the communist system and the ways and means of ensuring gradual movement towards its highest stage. An urgent task facing social sciences at the present stage is to provide the scientific analysis of the objective contradictions in socialist society, work out sound recommendations on how to overcome them, and make reliable economic and social forecasts.

The processes under way in the communist, working-class and national liberation movements, as well as in capitalist society should be studied most thoroughly. The course of world development confronts mankind with quite a few questions of global importance. Science should furnish correct answers to these questions. Combatting bourgeois ideology, revisionism and dogmatism has been and remains an important task of the social sciences.

The Party supports bold exploration, competition of ideas and trends in science, and fruitful discussion. Scholastic discourses and passive recording of facts which do not provide scope for daring conclusions of a general theoretical nature are alien to science, as are time-serving and loss of touch with reality. The complex and multifaceted problems of today call for a broader integration of the social, natural and technical sciences. Forms of organisation of science that provide for an interdisciplinary study of pressing problems, necessary mobility of scientific personnel and a flexible structure of scientific centres as well as effectiveness of research and development must be introduced on a greater scale. It is vital to enhance their role in the elaboration and fulfilment of plans for economic and social development. An indispensable condition for scientific progress is a constant influx of fresh forces, in particular from the sphere of production, efficient use of the creative potentialities of scientists, and active support of their work according to their actual contribution to solving theoretical and applied problems.

In the Field of Cultural Development, Literature and Art

The development of the multinational and truly popular Soviet culture, which has won worldwide recognition, is a historic achievement of our system. The great influence exercised by Soviet culture is due to its faithfulness to the truth of life and to the ideals of socialism and communism, to its profound humanism and optimism, and its close links with the people.

The CPSU attaches much importance to a fuller and deeper assimilation by working people of the values of intellectual and material culture and to their active involvement in artistic creative work. Steadily applying the Leninist principles of cultural development, the Party will see to the aesthetic education of the working people, in particular of the young generations, based on the best works of national and world artistic culture. Implementation of aesthetic principles will provide an even greater inspiration to work, raise the stature of man and enrich his everyday life.

The sphere of culture is called upon to meet the growing requirements of various sections of the population, to provide adequate opportunity for amateur artistic activity, to develop talents, to enrich the socialist way of life, and to mould healthy requirements and fine aesthetic values. For the successful accomplishment of these tasks, the Party considers it absolutely essential to improve the contents and methods of cultural work, strengthen the material base of this work and carry out intensive cultural development programmes in the countryside and newly-developed regions.

The Party will promote in every way the role of literature and art, which are called upon to serve the interests of the people and the cause of communism, to be a source of joy and inspiration for millions of people, to express their will, sentiments and thoughts, and actively contribute to their ideological development and moral education.

The main line of development of literature and art consists in strengthening ties with the life of the people, in a truthful and highly artistic representation of socialist reality, in an inspired and vivid portrayal of the new and advanced, and in an impassioned exposure of everything which hampers social progress.

The art of socialist realism is based on the principles of partisanship and kinship with the people. It combines bold innovation in truthful artistic representation of life with the use and development of all the progressive traditions of national and world culture. Workers in literature and art have broad scope for truly free creative endeavour, for the professional mastery and for further development of diverse forms, styles and genres of realism. As the cultural standards of the people rise, the influence of art on the life of society and on its moral and psychological climate is enhanced. This increases the cultural workers' responsibility for the ideological orientation of their creative effort and for the artistic impact of their work.

The CPSU takes a careful and respectful attitude to talent and artistic search. At the same time it has always fought and will continue to fight against the lack of ideological commitment, the lack of discrimination in matters relating to a world outlook and artistic dullness, relying in this on the unions of creative workers, public opinion and Marxist-Leninist literary and art criticism.

Soviet culture facilitates mutual understanding and the drawing together of peoples and vigorously participates in the struggle against the forces of imperialism, reaction and war. Embodying the ideological values and diversity of the intellectual life of socialist society and its humanism, it contributes to world culture and manifests itself more and more forcefully as a powerful factor in the cultural progress of mankind and as a prototype of future communist culture.

Part Three

The Tasks of the CPSU on the International Scene, in the Drive for Peace and Social Progress

The international policy of the CPSU is based on the humane nature of socialist society, which is free from exploitation and oppression and has no classes or social groups interested in unleashing war. It is inseparably linked with the basic, strategic tasks of the Party within the country and expresses the common aspiration of the Soviet people to engage in constructive work and to live in peace with all nations.

The main goals and directions of the international policy of the CPSU are:

– provision of international conditions favourable to the perfection of socialist society in the USSR and its advance to communism; removal of the threat of world war and achievement of universal security and disarmament;
– constant strengthening and expansion of cooperation between the USSR and the fraternal socialist countries and the utmost contribution to the consolidation and progress of the world socialist system;
– development of relations of equality and friendship with newly free countries;
– maintenance and development of relations between the USSR and capitalist states on a basis of peaceful coexistence and business-like, mutually beneficial cooperation;
– internationalist solidarity with Communist and revolutionary-democratic parties, the international working-class movement and the national liberation struggle of the peoples.

The CPSU's approach to foreign-policy matters consists in firm protection of the interests of the Soviet people and resolute opposition to the aggressive policy of imperialism combined with a readiness for dialogue and constructive settlement of international problems through negotiations.

The foreign-policy course for peace elaborated by the Party and consistently pursued by the Soviet state in combination with the strengthening of the defence capability of the country has ensured for the Soviet people and for most of the world's population the longest period of peace in the 20th century. The CPSU will continue to do everything it can to secure peaceful conditions for the constructive work of the Soviet people, to improve international relations, and to stop the arms race that has engulfed the world, in order to avert the danger of nuclear war, which looms over all peoples.

There is no loftier or more responsible mission than that of safeguarding and strengthening peace and curbing the forces of aggression and militarism for the sake of the life of present and future generations. **A world without wars and without weapons is the ideal of socialism.**

I. Cooperation with Socialist Countries

The CPSU attaches primary importance to the further development and strengthening of relations of friendship between the Soviet Union and other socialist countries.

The Party is seeking long-lasting comradely relations and many-sided cooperation between the USSR and all the other states of the world socialist system. The CPSU proceeds from the belief that the cohesion of the countries of socialism meets the interests of each of them and their common interests, and promotes the cause of peace and the triumph of socialist ideals.

The all-round strengthening of relations of friendship and the development and perfection of ties between the Soviet Union and the other countries of the socialist community are a matter of special concern to the Party.

The ruling Communist and Workers' parties are the motive force of these countries' all-round cooperation. To strengthen the cohesion of the Communists of the fraternal countries and to ensure mutual enrichment of the practice of guiding society, the CPSU will continue to help broaden the inter-Party links that embrace Party organisations at all levels, from Central Committees to primary Party organisations; it will promote exchanges of opinions and experience both on a bilateral and multilateral basis.

The CPSU will continue its policy of strengthening inter-state relations between the Soviet Union and other socialist countries, of affirming them in treaties and agreements, of developing contacts between the legislative bodies and between the public organisations of these countries, and of further stepping up their political cooperation in all forms.

Soviet Communists stand for the increasingly efficient interaction of the fraternal countries on the international scene with due regard for the situation and interests of each of them and for the common interests of the community.

As long as the imperialist NATO military bloc exists, the Party considers it necessary to help improve in every way possible the work of the Warsaw Treaty Organisation as an instrument of collective defence against the aggressive ambitions of imperialism and of joint struggle for a lasting peace and broader international cooperation.

In economic relations, the CPSU stands for a further deepening of socialist economic integration as the material foundation for drawing the socialist countries closer together. It attaches special importance to a consistent uniting of efforts by the fraternal countries in key areas of intensification of production and acceleration of scientific and technological progress in order to accomplish jointly a task of historical significance, namely, that of advancing to the fore-front of science and technology with the aim of further improving the well-being of their peoples and strengthening their security.

The Party proceeds from the belief that integration is designed to contribute to an ever increasing extent to progress in the sphere of social production and the socialist way of life in the countries of the socialist community, to evening out more rapidly their levels of economic development and to strengthening the positions of socialism in the world.

The CPSU will actively participate in the collective work of the fraternal parties to coordinate their economic policies, to improve the mechanism of their economic cooperation and evolve new forms of cooperation, to deepen specialisation and cooperation in production, to coordinate plans, to exchange advanced experience and to develop direct links between associations and enterprises. It will help enhance the role of the Council for Mutual Economic Assistance and broaden economic, scientific and technical cooperation on the basis of bilateral and multilateral-programmes.

While considering equal and mutually beneficial economic cooperation between socialist and capitalist states to be natural and useful, the CPSU at the same time believes that the development of socialist integration should enhance the technical and economic invulnerability of the community with regard to hostile actions by imperialism and to the influence of economic crises and other negative phenomena that are intrinsic to capitalism.

In the sphere of ideology, the CPSU stands for pooling the efforts of the fraternal parties aimed at studying and using the experience in building socialism and in the communist education of working people, at developing the theory of Marxism-Leninism while deepening its creative nature and upholding its revolutionary essence. An invigoration of collective thought, a constant widening of exchanges of cultural and intellectual values, and cooperation in science and culture serve further to strengthen friendship between socialist countries.

The Party will continue to enhance awareness of the unity and common historical destinies of the fraternal peoples. Propagation of the truth about socialism, exposure of imperialist policy and propaganda, rebuffing of anti-communism and anti-Sovietism, and struggle against dogmatic and revisionist views – these tasks are more easily accomplished when Communists act in a single front.

The CPSU regards it as its internationalist duty, together with the other fraternal parties, to consolidate the unity and increase the strength and influence of the socialist community. The outcome of the competition between socialism and capitalism and the future of world civilisation depend largely on the strength of the community, on the success of each country in its constructive endeavours, and on the purposefulness and coordination of their actions.

The experience of the development of the world socialist system shows that socialism provides every opportunity both for the society's confident advance and for the maintenance of harmonious mutual relations between countries. But neither comes of its own accord.

The levels of countries' economic and political development, their historical and cultural traditions, and the actual conditions in which they exist are different. The social development of socialist countries does not always proceed in a straightforward manner. Every major stage of this development sets new complex tasks, whose accomplishment involves struggle, search and the overcoming of contradictions and difficulties.

All this, the CPSU is convinced, calls for utmost attention, a constructive comparison of points of view and effective solidarity so as to rule out any possibility for the rise of differences that could harm common interests. Of special importance are the coordination of actions in matters of principle, comradely interest in each other's success, strict carrying out of commitments, and a profound understanding of both national interests and common, international interests in their organic interconnection.

The formation and development of a new society are taking place in a situation of sharp confrontation between the two world systems. Seeking to weaken the positions of socialism and disrupt the mutual ties of socialist states, and primarily ties with the Soviet Union, imperialism is employing a whole range of differentiated measures – political, economic and ideological. It tries to exploit problems that arise and makes use of nationalistic sentiments for subversive purposes. The CPSU proceeds from the belief that strong unity and class solidarity among socialist countries are especially important in these conditions.

The experience of the USSR, of world socialism shows that the most important factors in its successful advance are the loyalty of the ruling Communist and Workers' parties to the doctrine of Marxism-Leninism and a creative application of that doctrine; firm links between the parties and the broad mass of working people, an enhancing of the authority of the parties and their guiding role in society, strict observance of the Leninist norms of Party and state life, and development of government by the people under socialism; a sober consideration of the actual situation, timely and scientifically substantiated solution of problems that arise; and the building of relations with other fraternal countries on the principles of socialist internationalism.

Whatever the characteristic features of each of the socialist countries, its level of economic development, size, and historical and national traditions, all of them have the same class interests. What unites the socialist countries and makes them cohesive is of paramount importance and is immeasurably greater than what may divide them.

The CPSU is convinced that the socialist countries, fully observing the principles of equality and mutual respect for one another's national interests, will continue to follow the road of ever greater mutual understanding and will draw closer together. The Party will contribute to this historically progressive process.

II. Strengthening Relations with Newly Free Countries

Formulating its policy towards former colonial and semi-colonial countries, the CPSU proceeds from the belief that the embarking of the formerly enslaved peoples on the road of independence, the emergence of dozens of new states and their increasing role in world politics and in the world economy are one of the distinctive features of the present epoch.

The newly free peoples, as Lenin foresaw, are to play a great role in the destinies of mankind as a whole. **The CPSU believes that these peoples' increasing influence should promote to an ever greater extent the cause of peace and social progress.**

The Party is consistently pursuing a policy of expanding contacts between the Soviet Union and the newly free countries, and regards with profound sympathy the aspirations of the peoples who had experienced the heavy and humiliating yoke of colonial slavery. The Soviet Union is building its relations with those countries on the basis of strict respect for their independence and equality, and supports the struggle of those countries against the neo-colonialist policy of imperialism, against the survivals of colonialism, and for peace and universal security.

The Party attaches great importance to solidarity and political and economic cooperation with **socialist-oriented countries**. Every people creates, mostly by its own efforts, the material and technical base necessary for the building of a new society, and seeks to improve the well-being and cultural standards of the masses. The Soviet Union has been doing and will continue to do all it can to render the peoples following that road assistance in economic and cultural development, in training national personnel, in strengthening their defences and in other fields.

The CPSU is developing closer relations with the **revolutionary-democratic parties** of newly free countries. Especially close cooperation has been established with those of them that seek to base their activities on scientific socialism. The CPSU stands for the development of contacts with all national progressive parties holding anti-imperialist and patriotic positions.

Relations between the Soviet Union and newly free countries have demonstrated that there also exists a realistic basis for cooperation with those young states that are following the capitalist road of development. This basis consists in a common interest in safeguarding peace, strengthening international security and ending the arms race; in a sharpening contradiction between the interests of the peoples and the imperialist policy of diktat and expansion; and in an understanding by young states of the fact that political and economic ties with the Soviet Union help to strengthen their independence.

However different the newly free countries may be from one another and whatever road they follow, their peoples share a common desire to develop independently and to run their affairs without foreign interference. The Soviet Union is in full solidarity with them. The CPSU does not doubt that it is the sacred right of the newly free countries to decide their own destinies and to choose their own type of social system.

The CPSU supports the just struggle waged by the countries of Asia, Africa, and Latin America against imperialism and the oppression of transnational monopolies, for the assertion of the sovereign right to be master of one's own resources, for a restructuring of international relations on an equal and democratic basis, for the establishment of a new international economic order, and for the deliverance from the burden of debt imposed by the imperialists.

The Soviet Union is on the side of the states and peoples repulsing the attacks of the aggressive forces of imperialism and upholding their freedom, independence and national dignity. Solidarity with them in our time is also an important aspect of the general struggle for peace and international security. The Party regards it as its internationalist duty to support the struggle of the peoples who are still under the yoke of racism and who are victims of the system of apartheid.

The CPSU regards with understanding the goals and activities of the non-aligned movement and stands for an enhancement of its role in world politics. The USSR will continue to be on the side of the non-aligned states in their struggle against the forces of aggression and hegemonism and for settling disputes and conflicts that arise through negotiations, and will be opposed to the involvement of those states in military and political groupings.

The CPSU stands for the equal participation of newly free countries in international affairs and for an increase of their contribution to the solution of the most important problems of our time. The interaction of those countries with socialist states is vastly important for strengthening the independence of the peoples, improving international relations and preserving peace.

The alliance of the forces of social progress and national liberation is a guarantee of a better future for mankind.

III. Relations with Capitalist Countries. The Struggle for a Lasting Peace and Disarmament

The CPSU proceeds from the belief that the historical dispute between the two opposing social systems, into which the world is divided today, can and must be settled by peaceful means. Socialism proves its superiority not by force of arms, but by force of example in every area of the life of society – by the dynamic development of the economy, science and culture, by an improvement in the living standards of working people, and by a deepening of socialist democracy.

Soviet Communists are convinced that the future belongs to socialism. Every people deserves to live in a society that is free from social and national oppression, in a society of genuine equality and genuine democracy. It is the sovereign right of an oppressed and exploited people to free itself from exploitation and injustice. Revolutions are a natural outcome of social development, of class struggle in every given country. The CPSU believed and continues to believe that the 'export' of revolution, the imposition of revolution

100

on anyone from the outside, is unacceptable in principle. But the 'export' of counterrevolution in any form, too, is a gross encroachment on the free expression of will by the peoples, on their right independently to choose their way of development. The Soviet Union is strongly opposed to attempts forcibly to check and reverse the march of history.

The interests of the peoples demand that inter-state relations be directed onto a path of peaceful competition and equal cooperation.

The Communist Party of the Soviet Union firmly and consistently upholds the Leninist principle of peaceful coexistence of states with different social systems. The policy of peaceful coexistence as understood by the CPSU presupposes: renunciation of war and the use or threat of force as a means of settling disputed issues, and the settlement of such issues through negotiations; non-interference in internal affairs and respect for the legitimate interests of each other; the right of the peoples independently to decide their destinies; strict respect for the sovereignty and territorial integrity of states and the inviolability of their borders; cooperation on the basis of complete equality and mutual benefit; fulfilment in good faith of commitments arising from generally recognised principles and norms of international law and from international treaties concluded.

These are the basic principles on which the Soviet Union builds its relations with capitalist states. They have been affirmed in the Constitution of the USSR.

The CPSU will purposefully help to bring about a universal affirmation in international relations of the principle of peaceful coexistence as a generally recognised norm of inter-state relations that will be observed by everyone. It believes that the extension of ideological differences between the two systems to the sphere of inter-state relations is inadmissible.

The Party will work for the development of the process of international detente, regarding it as a natural and essential stage on the road to the establishment of a comprehensive and reliable security system. The experience of cooperation shows that there is a real prospect for this. The CPSU stands for the creation and use of international mechanisms and institutions that would make it possible to find optimal correlations between national, state interests and the common interests of mankind. It stands for enhancing the role of the United Nations in strengthening peace and developing international cooperation.

The nuclear powers bear a special responsibility for the situation in the world. The states possessing nuclear weapons and other weapons of mass destruction must renounce the use of or threat to use such weapons and refrain from steps that would lead to an aggravation of the international situation.

The CPSU stands for normal and stable relations between the Soviet Union and the United States of America, which presupposes non-interference in internal affairs, respect for each other's legitimate interests, recognition and practical implementation of the principle of equality and equal security, and the building of the greatest possible mutual trust on this basis. Differences between social systems and ideologies should not lead to strained relations. There are objective prerequisites for the development of fruitful and mutually beneficial Soviet-US cooperation in various fields. It is the conviction of the CPSU that the policies of both powers should be oriented to mutual understanding rather than hostility which is fraught with the threat of catastrophic consequences for the Soviet and American people as well as for other nations.

The Party is convinced that all states, big and small, regardless of their potentials, geographic location, and social systems, can and must participate in the search for solutions to acute problems, in the normalisation of conflict situations, and in carrying out measures to ease tensions and curb the arms race.

The CPSU attaches great importance to the further development of peaceful, good-neighbourly relations and cooperation between European states. An indispensable condition for the stability of positive processes in this region, as in other regions, is respect for the territorial and political realities which emerged as a result of the Second World War. The CPSU is strongly opposed to attempts to revise them under any pretext whatsoever and will combat any manifestation of revanchism.

The Party will make consistent efforts to ensure that the process of strengthening security, trust and peaceful cooperation in Europe, which was launched on the initiative and with the active participation of the Soviet Union, develops and deepens, and **comes to embrace the whole world.** The CPSU stands for the pooling of efforts by all interested states for the purpose of ensuring security in Asia and for carrying out a joint search by them for a constructive solution to the problem. Asia, Africa, Latin America, the Pacific and the Indian Oceans can and must become zones of peace and good-neighbourliness.

The CPSU stands for the development of extensive long-term and stable contacts between states in the sphere of the economy, science, and technology on the basis of complete equality and mutual benefit. Foreign economic cooperation is of great political importance, for it helps to strengthen peace and relations of peaceful coexistence between states with different social systems. The Soviet Union rejects all forms of discrimination and the use of trade, economic, scientific and technical contacts as a means of exerting pressure, and will work to ensure the economic security of states.

The CPSU stands for broad mutual exchanges of genuine cultural values between all countries. Such exchanges should serve humanitarian goals, namely, the cultural and intellectual enrichment of the peoples and the consolidation of peace and good-neighbourliness.

The Soviet state will cooperate with other countries in solving the global problems that have become especially acute in the second half of the 20th century and that are of vital significance to the whole of mankind. These include: environmental protection, energy, raw materials, food and demographic problems, peaceful exploration of outer space and the resources of the World Ocean, the overcoming of the economic backwardness of many newly free countries, the eradication of dangerous diseases, and other problems. The solution of these problems calls for joint efforts by all states. It will be much easier to solve these problems if the squandering of efforts and resources on the arms race is stopped.

In the interests of mankind and for the benefit of all nations, **the CPSU and the Soviet state stand for an extensive and constructive programme of measures aimed at ending the arms race, achieving disarmament, and ensuring peace and security.**

The CPSU, which considers **general and complete disarmament** under strict and comprehensive international control to be a historic task and is carrying out efforts to achieve it, shall consistently be working for:

– **restriction and narrowing of the sphere of military preparations**, especially those involving weapons of mass destruction. First and foremost, outer space should be totally excluded from that sphere so that it will not become the scene of military rivalry and a source of death and destruction. Exploration and development of outer space should be for peaceful purposes only, for the development of science and production, in accordance with the needs of all nations. The USSR stands for collective efforts in the solution of this problem and will actively participate in international cooperation to this end. The Soviet Union will also call for the adoption of measures promoting the non-proliferation of nuclear weapons and the establishment of zones free from these and other weapons of mass destruction;

– **the complete elimination of nuclear armaments** to be carried out stage by stage till the end of the 20th century by means of discontinuing the testing and production of all types of these armaments, renouncing the first use of nuclear weapons by all the nuclear powers, and freezing, reducing and destroying all their stockpiles;

– **an end to the production of other types of weapons of mass destruction**, including chemical weapons, **their elimination**, and a ban on the development of new types of such weapons;
– **reductions in the armed forces of states**, first and foremost those which are permanent members of the UN Security Council and countries that have military agreements with them; limitations on conventional armaments; an end to the development of new types of these armaments whose yield approximates that of mass destruction weapons, and reductions in military spending;
– **a freeze on, and reductions in, the number of troops and armaments in the most explosive parts of the world**, the dismantling of military bases on foreign territory, and measures to build up mutual trust and lessen the risk of armed conflicts, including those that might occur by accident.

The CPSU stands for overcoming the division of the world into military-political groupings. The CPSU is for simultaneous dissolution of NATO and the Warsaw Treaty Organisation, or, as a first step, the disbandment of their military organisations. To lower confrontation between the military blocs, the Soviet Union advocates the conclusion of a treaty between them on the mutual non-use of force and the maintenance of relations of peace, a treaty which would be open to all other states as well.

The Party will make every effort to ensure that questions of arms limitation and averting the threat of war are tackled through honest and strictly observed agreements on the basis of equality and equal security of the sides, in order to preclude any attempt to conduct talks from a 'position of strength' and use them to cover up an arms buildup.

The Soviet state and its allies do not seek military superiority, but at the same time they will not permit an upset in the military-strategic equilibrium that has taken shape in the world arena. Furthermore, they are consistently working to ensure that the level of this equilibrium is steadily lowered, the quantity of armaments on both sides reduced, and the security of all peoples guaranteed.

The CPSU solemnly declares: there are no weapons that the Soviet Union would not be prepared to limit or ban on a reciprocal basis with effective verification.

The USSR does not encroach on the security of any country, West or East. It threatens no one and does not seek confrontation with any state; it wishes to live in peace with all countries. The Soviet socialist state has been bearing high the banner of peace and friendship among peoples since the Great October Revolution. The CPSU shall remain loyal to this Leninist banner.

IV. The CPSU in the International Working-Class and Communist Movement

The CPSU is a component part of the international communist movement. It regards its efforts to perfect socialist society and advance onward to communism as a major internationalist task, the accomplishment of which serves the interests of the world socialist system, the international working class, and mankind as a whole.

Communists, having always been the most consistent fighters against social and national oppression, are today also in the forefront of the struggle for the preservation of peace on earth and for people's right to life. They know well wherein lie the causes of the threat of war, expose those who are responsible for the aggravation of international tension and the arms race, and strive to develop cooperation with all those capable of making a contribution to the anti-war effort.

The CPSU takes into consideration the fact that Communist and Workers' parties in the non-socialist world are functioning in a complex and controversial situation. The range of the circumstances and forms of their struggle is quite broad. However, this expands rather than limits the opportunities available to the movement. The diversity of forms of activity practised by Communists enables them to take better account of specific national conditions and concrete historical circumstances, and of the interests of different social groups and strata of the population.

The CPSU proceeds from the conviction that the Communists in each country independently analyse and evaluate situations and determine their strategic course, policies and means of struggle for the immediate and ultimate goals, for communist ideals. The experience accumulated by the Communist parties is a valuable internationalist asset.

The CPSU thoroughly studies the problems and experience of foreign Communist parties. It regards with understanding their desire to improve their strategy and tactics, to seek broader class alliances on a platform of anti-monopolistic, anti-war activity, and to uphold the economic interests and political rights of working people, proceeding from the conviction that the struggle for democracy is a component part of the struggle for socialism.

The imperialist circles in different countries are closely coordinating their efforts aimed against socialism and all the democratic forces and are trying to set Communist parties against one another. In these conditions proletarian internationalism and comradely solidarity among Communists are assuming ever greater importance.

The CPSU believes that disagreement over individual issues should not interfere with international cooperation among Communist parties and their concerted efforts.

In cases when divergences of views on individual problems arise between fraternal parties, the CPSU considers it useful to hold comradely discussions to achieve better understanding of each other's views and reach mutually acceptable appraisals. But when the issue at hand is the revolutionary essence of Marxism-Leninism, the substance and role of real socialism, the CPSU will continue to uphold positions of principle. This also determines the CPSU's attitude to all attempts to destroy the class essence of the Communists' activity and distort the revolutionary nature of the aims and means of struggle for attaining them. Experience has shown that any departure from the fundamental propositions of the teaching of Marx, Engels, and Lenin weakens the potentials of the communist movement.

In its relations with the fraternal parties, **the CPSU firmly adheres to the principle of proletarian internationalism**, which organically combines revolutionary solidarity with the recognition of the full independence and equality of each party. On the basis of this principle, the CPSU is actively developing its ties with the Communist and Workers' parties, exchanging information, and participating in bilateral and multilateral meetings and regional and broader international conferences held as the need arises.

Soviet Communists always side with their class comrades in the capitalist world. The CPSU will use its international prestige to defend Communists who fall victim to the arbitrary rule of reactionaries. It has a high regard for the solidarity of the fraternal parties and for their struggle against anti-Sovietism. The mutual support of the Communist and Workers' parties in the socialist and non-socialist countries is an important factor for social progress.

The CPSU will continue its policy of developing ties with socialist, social-democratic, and labour parties. Cooperation with them can play a significant role, first and foremost, in the effort to prevent nuclear war. However great the divergences between various trends of the working-class movement might be, they present no obstacle to a fruitful and systematic exchange of views, parallel or joint actions to remove the threat of war, improve the international situation, eliminate the vestiges of colonialism, and uphold the interests and rights of the working people.

The Party attaches great significance to stimulating cooperation among all contingents of the international working-class movement and expanding interaction between trade unions of diverse trends and youth, women's, peasant and other democratic organisations in various countries.

Being fully aware of its historical responsibility to the world's working class and its communist vanguard, the CPSU will continue to work in the following directions:

– to uphold the revolutionary ideals and the fundamentals of Marxism-Leninism in the world communist movement, creatively develop the theory of scientific socialism, consistently fight against dogmatism and revisionism, against all the influences of bourgeois ideology on the working-class movement;
– to do its utmost to promote cohesion and cooperation among fraternal parties and the international solidarity of Communists and to increase the communist movement's contribution to the cause of preventing world war;
– to pursue a consistent policy aimed at achieving unity of action in the international working-class movement, among all working people in the struggle for their common interests, for a lasting peace and the security of peoples, for national independence, democracy, and socialism.

Part Four

The CPSU – The Leading Force in Soviet Society

The Communist Party of the Soviet Union has traversed a path that is unprecedented in its depth and force of impact on social development. Its ascent has been swift: from the first Marxist circles through three people's revolutions to the leadership of a great socialist power.

The historic achievements of the Soviet people in building a new society, their victory in the Great Patriotic War, the country's confident advance towards ever higher stages of socio-economic and cultural progress, and the growth of the Soviet Union's influence on the course of world development are inseparably linked with the Communist Party's activities. It is the inspirer and organiser of the historical creative activity of the people, our society's leading and guiding force. Equipped with Marxist-Leninist theory, the Party is determining the general prospects for the country's development, ensuring a science-based leadership of the creative activities of the people, and lending an organised, plan-based, and purposeful character to the building of communism.

As a result of the fact that socialism has been built in the USSR, that all sections of the working people have gone over to the positions of the working class, and that the socio-political and ideological unity of Soviet society has been consolidated, the Communist Party, while retaining its class essence and ideology as the party of the working class, has become the party of all the people. This predetermines the revolutionary continuity, the class character of domestic and foreign policy, and the entire activity of the CPSU.

In the new historical conditions, when the country is confronted with important tasks in its internal development and in the international arena, the **Party's leading role** in the life of Soviet society **inevitably grows**, and higher demands are made on the level of its political, organisational ideological activity. This is predetermined by the following essential factors:

– growth in the scale and complexity of the tasks of perfecting socialism and accelerating the country's socio-economic development; the need to elaborate and implement consistently a policy that ensures the successful fulfilment of these tasks and an organic interconnection between the economic, social, and cultural progress of society;

– development of the political system, strengthening democracy and socialist self-government by the people by enhancing the political and labour enthusiasm of the masses, extensively drawing them into administering production and state and public affairs;

– the need for further creative development of Marxist-Leninist theory, a profound comprehension of the experience of building communism, a search for science-based and timely answers to the questions posed by life, raising the social consciousness of the working people, and elimination of the manifestations of petty-bourgeois mentality and ethics and all deviations from the norms of the socialist way of life;

– interest in deepening all-round cooperation, strengthening the unity of the socialist countries and the international communist and working-class movement, solidarity with the forces of national liberation, and the struggle against bourgeois ideology, revisionism, dogmatism, reformism, and sectarianism;

– complication of foreign-policy conditions in connection with the growing aggressiveness of imperialism, the need to be more vigilant, to assure the country's security and to make new, increasingly persistent efforts to curb the forces of aggression, stop the arms race, rid mankind of the threat of nuclear catastrophe and strengthen peace on earth.

In carrying out the political leadership of society, the CPSU will continue consistently **to apply the time-tested Leninist principles, assert the Leninist style** in Party work, all fields of administration of the state and the economy, enhance the science-based nature of its policy; the Party will rely extensively on the collective wisdom and experience of the people and will develop their social initiative. It attaches fundamental significance to the unity of ideological-theoretical, political-educational, organisational and economic activity, to the uncompromising struggle against any stagnation and conservatism, to the creative quest for effective solutions to problems that arise.

The CPSU considers it necessary to take careful account of the specific character of the functions of Party, state and public bodies, to coordinate their work, to avoid duplication of activities, to enhance the role of the Party Committees as bodies of political leadership, to eliminate manifestations of formalism and red tape, bureaucratic and other distortions in the work of the administrative apparatus, to intensify control over the fulfilment of Party decisions and economic plans, to strengthen state and labour discipline and order, and to raise organisational standards.

In the activity of all Party organisations and work collectives, the CPSU will persistently instill a creative attitude, efficiency, high responsibility and adherence to principles, as well as an ability to evaluate the results attained objectively and self-critically, to be attentive and sensitive towards people, their needs and requirements.

The Party inseparably links the higher standards in the guidance of state, economic, and cultural development with further **improvement in working with personnel**. It considers it vital that the Leninist principles of selecting and evaluating personnel on the basis of political, business, and moral qualities be strictly observed everywhere from top to bottom, and that public opinion be given even greater consideration.

By its entire personnel policy the CPSU will facilitate the promotion to leadership positions of Communists and non-Party people who are politically mature, possess high moral standards, are competent and full of initiative; the Party will be more active in advancing women to positions of leadership. The Party attaches fundamental importance to such qualities in a leader as responsiveness to new ideas, closeness to people, readiness to undertake responsibility, a desire to learn to work better, an ability to understand the political meaning of economic management, and high demands on one's self and on others.

The Party sees to it that young, promising workers work side by side with members of the older generation who are more experienced so that they might gain experience and the necessary training. This is a natural process which provides a reliable guarantee against inertia, stagnation, and voluntarism.

Confidence in personnel must be combined with exactingness, with their greater personal responsibility to Party organisations and work collectives for the results of work and maintenance of Party and state discipline, and with stricter control by the people over the activity of managers. Each manager should be fully accountable for the work entrusted to him. He should establish proper relations with people and inspire them by personal example. **No Party organisation, no one should remain outside the sphere of control.**

The development of the Party is characterised by a **further growth and strengthening of Party ranks, and an improvement in inner-Party relations on the principle of democratic centralism.**

Filling its ranks with the foremost representatives of the working class, collective-farm peasantry, and the Soviet intelligentsia, the Party increases its influence in various fields of building communism. The CPSU considers it essential that industrial workers hold a leading place in its social composition. A person's political and business qualities, honesty and decency, readiness to devote all his or her energies to the cause of communism remain the decisive condition for admission to the Party. Attempts to join the Party in order to make a career should be stopped immediately.

Party membership gives no privileges; it implies only an even higher responsibility for all that takes place within the country, for the destiny of building communism and social progress. Every Communist must be exemplary in work and behaviour, in public and personal life. The strength of the Party's links with the masses, its prestige among them depends in large measure on how fully the **vanguard role of the Communists** manifests itself. The Party will steadily raise its demands on each Communist concerning his or her attitude to duty and the honest and pure moral make-up of the Party member; it will appraise each member by his or her work and deeds.

The CPSU believes that a guarantee of the successful activity and of high creative enthusiasm of the Communists lies in further **developing and deepening inner-Party democracy**, in strictly observing the Leninist norms of Party life, in promoting criticism and self-criticism, in ensuring greater openness and publicity.

The Party will continue to base its work on the tested **principle of collectivity**. To ensure its further implementation and development, the CPSU considers it essential to enhance the role and significance of Party meetings, plenary meetings, conferences and congresses, and of Party committees and bureaus as collective bodies of leadership, and to provide favourable conditions for a free and businesslike discussion in the Party of questions relating to its policy and practical activity.

While working for the consistent practical implementation of the democratic principles of inner-Party life, the CPSU simultaneously devotes unremitting attention to **strengthening Party discipline**. Firm, conscious discipline on the part of Party members is a necessary prerequisite for high socialist discipline in all spheres of public life.

Successful Party activity and the growth of enthusiasm of the Communists are inseparably linked with a further improvement in the work of the Party's primary organisations. Since they are the political nucleus of work collectives, they are called upon to contribute in every way possible to bringing about the unity of the Party's policy and the vital creative activity of the people.

The Party will always strengthen the unity and monolithic cohesion of its ranks. It preserves in its arsenal of means the organisational guarantees envisaged in the CPSU Rules against any manifestation of factionalism and cliquishness. **The most important source of the Party's strength and invincibility is the indestructible ideological and organisational cohesion of the Party.**

The CPSU proceeds from the Marxist-Leninist proposition that people are the makers of history, and that the building of communism is the work of their hands, energy, and minds. The vital creative activity of the people is the guarantee of all our achievements.

The Party exists for the people and sees the meaning of its activity in service to the people. The goals and tasks it sets itself are an expression of the aspirations and vital interests of the Soviet people. The Party will continue to work in a spirit of high responsibility to the people, constantly broadening and deepening its links with them and showing understanding for people's needs and concerns. It regards as its duty constantly to consult working people on key issues of domestic and foreign policy, carefully take into account public opinion, and draw non-Party people on an ever broader scale into the work of Party organisations. The more actively the Party is supported by the people, the more it influences the course of social development.

In all of its activity the CPSU is invariably guided by the **time-tested Marxist-Leninist principles of proletarian, socialist internationalism.** It will contribute in every way possible to promoting the cohesion of the international communist movement on the basis of Marxism-Leninism, develop fraternal ties with all the Communist and Workers' parties, actively cooperate with them in the struggle for peace and against the danger of a nuclear catastrophe, and support their struggle in defence of the vital interests of the working people, for national liberation, democracy and socialism.

* * *

This is the Programme of the Communist Party of the Soviet Union.

The Party calls upon all the Communists, all working people – workers, collective farmers, and members of the intelligentsia – to take a most vigorous part in the implementation of the historical tasks set forth in the Programme. The Party is confident that Soviet people, regarding the Programme of the CPSU as their vital cause, will make every effort to implement it.

To achieve a qualitatively new state of society by substantially accelerating socio-economic progress – this is the Party strategy. The all-round perfection of socialism will bring new benefits to every family, to every Soviet citizen. It will lead to a further flourishing of our socialist homeland and, finally, to the triumph of communism.

The onward march of our people to this cherished goal will increase the attractive force of the ideas of Marxism-Leninism, of transforming society on the principles of humanism and social justice. They win the minds and hearts of people by providing an example of better social organisation, a steady growth of productive forces, by ensuring conditions for creative work, for people's happiness, and well-being, resolutely rejecting wars of aggression, and affirming the principles of peace and broad cooperation between peoples on the basis of equality and universal security.

Communists, all the working people of our country, are looking optimistically to the future. The Party is firmly convinced that by the selfless labour effort of the Soviet people, a creator and builder, the tasks set will be accomplished and the goals outlined achieved.

Under the leadership of the Party, under the banner of Marxism-Leninism the Soviet people have built socialism.

Under the leadership of the Party, under the banner of Marxism-Leninism the Soviet people will build a communist society.

Rules of the Communist Party of the Soviet Union

Approved by the 27th Congress of the CPSU on March 1, 1986

Rules of the Communist Party of the Soviet Union

The Communist Party of the Soviet Union is the tried and tested militant vanguard of the Soviet people, which unites, on a voluntary basis, the more advanced, politically more conscious section of the working class, collective-farm peasantry and intelligentsia of the USSR.

Founded by V.I. Lenin as the advance detachment of the working class, the Communist Party has travelled a glorious road of struggle. It brought the working class and the working peasantry to the victory of the Great October Socialist Revolution and to the establishment of the dictatorship of the proletariat in our country. Under the leadership of the Communist Party, the exploiting classes were abolished in the Soviet Union, and the socio-political and ideological unity of multinational Soviet society has taken shape and is steadily growing in strength. Socialism has triumphed completely and finally. The proletarian state has grown into a state of the entire people. The country has entered the stage of developed socialism.

Remaining in its class essence and ideology the Party of the working class, the CPSU has become the Party of the entire people.

The Party exists for and serves the people. It is the highest form of socio-political organization, the nucleus of the political system and the leading and guiding force of Soviet society. The Party defines the general perspective of the country's development, ensures the scientific guidance of the people's creative activities, and imparts an organized, planned and purposeful character to their struggle to achieve the ultimate goal, the victory of communism.

In all its activities, the CPSU is guided by Marxist-Leninist theory and its own Programme, which defines the tasks of the steady and all-round advancement of socialism and of the further progress of Soviet society towards communism on the basis of the country's accelerated socio-economic development.

The CPSU bases its work on unswerving adherence to the Leninist standards of Party life, the principles of democratic centralism, collective leadership, the comprehensive development of inner-Party democracy, the creative activity of Communists, criticism and self-criticism and broad publicity.

Ideological and organizational unity, monolithic cohesion of its ranks, and a high degree of conscious discipline on the part of all Communists are inviolable laws for the CPSU. Any manifestation of factionalism or group activity is incompatible with Marxist-Leninist Party principles, and with Party membership. The Party expels persons who violate the Programme and the Rules of the CPSU and compromise the worthy name of Communist by their behaviour.

In creatively developing Marxism-Leninism, the CPSU vigorously combats any manifestation of revisionism and dogmatism, which are utterly alien to revolutionary theory.

The Communist Party of the Soviet Union is an integral part of the international communist movement. It firmly adheres to the tried and tested Marxist-Leninist principles of proletarian, socialist internationalism, actively promotes the cooperation and cohesion of the fraternal socialist countries, of the world system of socialism, and the international communist and working class movement, and shows solidarity with the nations fighting for national and social liberation, against imperialism and for peace.

I. Party Members, Their Duties and Rights

1. Membership of the CPSU is open to any citizen of the Soviet Union who accepts the Programme and the Rules of the Party, takes an active part in communist construction, works in one of the Party organizations, carries out Party decisions, and pays membership dues.

2. It is the duty of a Party member:

(a) to implement, firmly and undeviatingly, the Party's general line and directives, to explain to the masses the CPSU's home and foreign policy, to organize the working people for its implementation, and to work for the strengthening and expansion of the Party's ties with the people;

(b) to set a good example at work, to protect and augment socialist property, to work persistently for higher production efficiency, for a steady growth of labour productivity, for higher product quality, for the application of the achievements of modern science and technology and advanced experience in the national economy; to upgrade his professional skills, to actively champion all that is new and progressive, to make the maximum possible contribution to the acceleration of the country's socio-economic development;

(c) to be active in the country's political life, in running state and public affairs, to set an example in fulfilling one's civic duty, to contribute actively to the ever fuller implementation of the people's socialist self-government;

(d) to master Marxist-Leninist theory, to widen his political and cultural horizons, and promote in all possible ways the growth of the Soviet people's consciousness and their ideological and moral standards. To combat resolutely any manifestations of bourgeois ideology, private-property mentality, religious prejudices and other views and morals alien to the socialist way of life;

(e) to abide strictly by the standards of communist morality, to assert the principle of social justice which is innate in socialism, to put public interests above personal, to be modest and upright, responsive and considerate to people, to respond promptly to working people's requirements and needs, to be truthful and honest with the Party and the people;

(f) to disseminate steadily the ideas of proletarian, socialist internationalism and Soviet patriotism among the working masses, to combat manifestations of nationalism and chauvinism, to work actively for the consolidation of friendship between the peoples of the USSR and fraternal relations with the countries of socialism, with the proletarians and working people of the whole world;

(g) to help in every possible way to strengthen the defence capability of the USSR; to struggle indefatigably for peace and friendship among nations;

(h) to strengthen the ideological and organizational unity of the Party, to safeguard the Party against infiltration by people who do not deserve the worthy name of Communist, to display vigilance, to keep Party and state secrets;

(i) to develop criticism and self-criticism, boldly expose shortcomings and work for their removal, to combat ostentation, conceit, complacency, and eyewash, to counter firmly all attempts at suppressing criticism, to combat bureaucracy, parochialism and departmentalism and all actions injurious to the Party and the state and to inform of them Party bodies, up to and including the CC CPSU;

(j) to pursue undeviatingly the Party's policy with regard to the proper selection of personnel according to their political, professional and moral qualities. To be uncompromising whenever the Leninist principles of the selection and education of personnel are violated;

(k) to observe Party and state discipline, which is equally binding on all Party members. The Party has one discipline, one law for all Communists, irrespective of their past services or the positions they occupy.

3. A Party member has the right:

(a) to elect and be elected to Party bodies;

(b) to discuss freely questions of the Party's policies and practical activities at Party meetings, conferences and congresses, at the meetings of Party committees and in the Party press, to put forward proposals; to express openly and uphold his opinion until the Party organization concerned adopts a decision;

(c) to criticize any Party body and any Communist, irrespective of the position he holds, at Party meetings, conferences and congresses, and at the plenary meetings of Party committees. Those who suppress criticism or victimize anyone for criticism shall be penalized strictly by the Party, to the point of expulsion from the CPSU;

(d) to attend in person all Party meetings and all bureau and committee sittings that discuss his activities or conduct;

(e) to address any question, statement or proposal to any Party body, up to and including the CC CPSU, and to demand an answer on the substance of his address.

4. Applicants are admitted to Party membership only individually. Membership of the Party is open to politically conscious and active citizens from among workers, peasants and the intelligentsia, all devoted to the communist cause. New members are admitted from among the candidate members who have undergone the established probationary period.

Persons may join the Party on reaching the age of eighteen. Young people up to the age of twenty-five may join the Party only through the All-Union Leninist Young Communist League (YCL).

The procedure for the admission of candidate members to full Party membership is as follows:

(a) Applicants for Party membership must submit recommendations from three members of the CPSU who have a Party standing of not less than five years and who know the applicants from having worked with them, professionally and socially, for not less than one year.[1,2]

---

1. In the case of members of the YCL applying for membership of the Party, the recommendation of a district or city committee of the YCL is equivalent to the recommendation of one Party member.

2. Members and alternate members of the CC CPSU refrain from giving recommendations.

(b) Applications for Party membership are discussed and a decision is taken by the general meeting of the primary Party organization; the decision of the latter is valid if not less than two-thirds of the Party members attending the meeting have voted for it, and comes into effect after endorsement by the district Party committee, or by the city Party committee in cities with no district division.

The question of admission to the Party may be discussed in the absence of those who have recommended the applicant for Party membership. Admission to the Party takes place, as a rule, at open meetings.

(c) Citizens of the USSR who formerly belonged to the Communist or Workers' Party of another country are admitted to membership of the Communist Party of the Soviet Union in conformity with the rules established by the CC CPSU.

5. Communists recommending applicants for Party membership are responsible to Party organizations for the impartiality of their description of the political, professional and moral qualities of those they recommend and help the latter further develop their ideological and political awareness.

6. The Party standing of those admitted to Party membership dates from the day the general meeting of the primary Party organization decides to accept them as full members.

7. The procedure of registering members and candidate members of the Party, and their transfer from one organization to another is determined by the appropriate instructions of the CC CPSU.

8. If a Party member or candidate member fails to pay membership dues for three months in succession without a good enough reason, the matter shall be discussed by the primary Party organization. If it is revealed as a result that the Party member or candidate member in question has virtually lost contact with the Party organization, he shall be regarded as having ceased to be a member of the Party; the primary Party organization shall pass a decision thereon and submit it to the district or city committee of the Party for endorsement.

9. A Party member or candidate member who fails to fulfil his duties as laid down in the Rules, or commits other offences, shall be called to account, and may incur a penalty: a warning, reprimand (severe reprimand) or a reprimand (severe reprimand) with note of this made in his registration card. The strictest Party penalty is expulsion from the Party.

In the case of minor offences, Party education measures and influence should be applied – in the form of comradely criticism, Party censure, warning or reproof.

A Communist who has committed an offence shall answer for it, above all, to his primary Party organization. The primary Party organization will be informed should a Communist be called to account to the Party by a higher body.

Maximum attention must be given to discussion of the question of calling a Party member to Party account and the grounds for the charges preferred against him must be thoroughly investigated.

The Party organization gives the Party member a hearing, not later than a year after the penalty was imposed on him, to find out how he is rectifying his shortcomings.

10. The decision to expel a Communist from the Party is made at the general meeting of a primary Party organization. The decision of the primary Party organization to expel a member is adopted provided not less than two-thirds of the Party members attending the meeting vote for it, and takes effect after endorsement by the district or city Party committee.

Until the decision to expel the member is endorsed by the district or city Party committee, the Party member or candidate member retains his membership card and is entitled to attend closed Party meetings.

A person expelled from the Party retains the right to appeal, within two months, to the higher Party bodies, up to and including the CC CPSU.

11. The question of calling to Party account a member or alternate member of the CC of the Communist Party of a Union Republic or of a territorial, regional, area, city or district Party committee, as well as a member of an auditing commission, is discussed by primary Party organizations and decisions to impose penalties are passed in conformity with the regular procedure.

Party organizations' proposals for expelling a Communist from the CPSU are reported to the relevant Party committee of which he is a member. The decision to expel from the Party a member or alternate member of the CC of the Communist Party of a Union Republic or of a territorial, regional, area, city or district Party committee, or a member of an auditing commission, is adopted at the plenary meeting of the committee concerned by a majority of two-thirds of the membership.

The decision to expel from the Party a member or alternate member of the Central Committee of the CPSU, or a member of the Central Auditing Commission of the CPSU, is adopted by the Party congress, and in the interim between congresses, by a plenary meeting of the Central Committee by a majority of two-thirds of the CC CPSU members.

12. A Party member shall bear dual responsibility to the state and the Party for the violation of Soviet laws. Persons who have

committed indictable offences are expelled from the CPSU.

13. Appeals by persons expelled or disciplined, as well as the decisions of Party organizations on expulsion from the Party, shall be examined by the appropriate Party bodies within not more than two months from the date of their receipt.

II. Candidate Members

14. All persons joining the Party must go through a probationary period as candidate members in order to familiarize themselves more thoroughly with the Programme and the Rules of the CPSU and prepare for admission to full membership. Party organizations must assist candidates to prepared for admission to full membership, and test their personal qualities in practical deeds, in the fulfilment of Party and public assignments.

The period of probationary membership shall be one year.

15. The admission procedure for candidate members (individual admission, submission of recommendations, decision of the primary organization on admission, and its endorsement) is identical with the admission procedure for Party members.

16. On the expiry of the candidate's probationary period the primary Party organization discusses his admission to full membership and passes a decision on it. Should a candidate member fail to prove worthy during the probationary period, and should that candidate member's personal traits rule out admission to membership of the CPSU, the Party organization shall pass a decision denying him admission to membership of the Party; after endorsement of that decision by the district or city Party committee, he shall cease to be considered a candidate member of the CPSU.

17. Candidate members of the Party participate in all the activities of their Party organizations; they shall have a consultative voice at Party meetings. Candidate members of the Party may not be elected to any leading Party body, nor may they be elected delegates to a Party conference or congress.

18. Candidate members of the CPSU pay membership dues at the same rate as full members.

III. Organizational Structure of the Party. Inner-party Democracy

19. The guiding principle of the organizational structure, of the life and activities of the Party is democratic centralism, which signifies:

(a) election of all leading Party bodies, from the lowest to the highest;

(b) periodical reports of Party bodies to their Party organizations and to higher bodies;

(c) strict Party discipline and subordination of the minority to the majority;

(d) the obligatory nature of the decisions of higher bodies for lower bodies;

(e) collective spirit in the work of all organizations and leading Party bodies and the personal responsibility of every Communist for the fulfilment of his duties and Party assignments.

20. The Party is built on the territorial and production principle: primary organizations are established wherever Communists are employed, and are associated territorially in district, city, etc., organizations. An organization uniting the Communists of a given area is higher than any component Party organization of that area.

21. All Party organizations are autonomous in deciding local questions, unless their decisions contradict Party policy.

22. The highest leading body of a Party organization is the general meeting or conference (for primary organizations), conference (for district, city, area, regional and territorial organizations), or congress (for Communist Parties of the Union Republics and the Communist Party of the Soviet Union). A meeting, conference or congress is considered competent if it is attended by more than one half of the members of the Party organization or of the elected delegates.

23. The general meeting, conference or congress elects a bureau or committee which acts as its executive body and directs all the current work of the Party organization.

An apparatus is set up at the CC CPSU, the CCs of the Communist Parties of the Union Republics, territorial, regional, area, city and district Party committees, for carrying out the current work of organizing and checking up on the fulfilment of Party decisions and rendering assistance to the lower organizations in their activities.

The CPSU Central Committee defines the structure and the staff of the Party apparatus.

24. Party bodies are elected by secret ballot. Elections of the secretaries, deputy secretaries of Party organizations and Party group organizers at meetings of primary, shop organizations with less than 15 Party members and of Party groups may be held, with the Communists' consent, by a show of hands. In these primary organizations, the procedure for the election of delegates to the district and city Party conferences is the same.

During elections all Party members have the unlimited right to challenge candidates and to criticize them. Each candidate shall be voted upon separately. A candidate is elected if more than one half of those attending the meeting, conference or congress vote for him.

The principle of the systematic renewal of the composition of Party bodies and of the continuity of leadership shall be observed in the election of all Party bodies – from primary organizations to the CPSU Central Committee.

25. The members and alternate members of the CC CPSU, the Central Committees of the Communist Parties of the Union Republics, the territorial, regional, area, city and district Party committees must, by their entire activity, justify the great trust placed in them. A member or alternate member of the Party committee who degrades his honour and dignity may not remain on the committee.

The question of removing a member or alternate member of a Party committee from that body is decided by a plenary meeting of the given committee. The decision is adopted if not less than two-thirds of the members of the Party committee have voted for it by secret ballot.

The question of removing members of the CPSU Central Auditing Commission, or of the auditing commissions of local Party organizations from these commissions is decided by their meetings according to the procedure established for members and alternate members of Party committees.

26. The free and effective discussion of questions of Party policy in the Party, in all its organizations, is an important principle of inner-Party democracy. Only on the basis of inner-Party democracy is it possible to ensure Communists' high creative activity, open criticism and self-criticism and strong Party discipline, which must be conscious and not mechanical.

Discussion of controversial or insufficiently clear issues may be held within the framework of individual organizations or the Party as a whole.

Party-wide discussion is held:

(a) on the initiative of the CC CPSU, if it considers it necessary to take counsel with the Party as a whole on a particular question of policy;

(b) at the proposal of several Party organizations at republican, territorial or regional level.

Broad discussion, especially discussion on a country-wide scale, of questions of Party policy must be so held as to ensure the free expression of Party members' views and preclude attempts to form factional groupings, to split the Party.

27. The supreme principle of Party leadership is collective leadership, which is an absolute requisite for the normal functioning of

Party organizations, the proper education of cadres, the promotion of the activity and initiative of Communists, and a reliable guarantee against the adoption of volitional, subjectivist decisions, the manifestation of the cult of the individual and violations of the Leninist principles of Party life.

Collective leadership implies personal responsibility for the matter in hand, constant control over the activities of every Party organization, every worker.

28. The CC CPSU, the Central Committees of the Communist Parties of the Union Republics, and territorial, regional, area, city and district Party committees shall systematically inform Party organizations, in the interim between congresses and conferences, of their work and of the actions taken on the strength of critical remarks and proposals made by Communists.

It is an unbreakable rule for the Party committees, primary Party organizations to objectively and promptly inform the higher Party bodies of their activities and the state of affairs in their organizations.

29. Meetings of the active of district, city, area, regional and territorial Party organizations and of the Communist Parties of the Union Republics shall be held to discuss major decisions of the Party and to work out measures for their implementation, as well as to examine questions of local significance.

30. Standing or temporary commissions and working groups on various questions of Party work may be set up at the Party committees, and other forms can also be used to draw Communists into the activities of the Party bodies on a voluntary basis.

IV. Higher Party Bodies

31. The supreme body of the Communist Party of the Soviet Union is the Party Congress. Regular congresses shall be convened by the Central Committee not less than once in five years. The convocation of the Party Congress and its agenda shall be announced at least six weeks before the Congress.

Extraordinary (emergency) congresses shall be convened by the Central Committee of the Party on its own initiative or on the demand of not less than one-third of the total Party membership represented at the preceding Party Congress. Extraordinary (emergency) congresses shall be convened within two months and are considered competent provided not less than one half of the total Party membership is represented at them.

The rates of representation at a Party Congress are determined by the Central Committee.

32. Should the Central Committee of the Party fail to convene an extraordinary (emergency) congress within the period specified in Article 31, the organizations which demanded its convocation have the right to form an Organizing Committee, which shall enjoy the powers of the Central Committee of the Party, for the convocation of the extraordinary (emergency) congress.

33. The Congress:

(a) hears and approves the reports of the Central Committee, of the Central Auditing Commission, and of the other central organizations;

(b) reviews, amends and approves the Programme and the Rules of the Party;

(c) determines the line of the Party in matters of home and foreign policy, and examines and decides the most important questions of Party and state life, of communist construction;

(d) elects the Central Committee and the Central Auditing Commission.

34. The number of members to be elected to the Central Committee and to the Central Auditing Commission is determined by the Congress. Vacancies arising in the Central Committee are filled from among the alternate members of the CC CPSU.

35. In the interim between congresses, the Central Committee of the Communist Party of the Soviet Union guides the entire activity of the Party and the local Party bodies, selects and appoints leading functionaries, directs the work of central government bodies and public organizations of working people, sets up various Party bodies, institutions and enterprises and guides their activities, appoints the editors of the central newspapers and journals operating under its control, and distributes the funds of the Party budget and controls its execution.

The Central Committee represents the CPSU in its relations with other parties.

36. The Central Auditing Commission of the CPSU verifies the observance of the established procedure for handling affairs, the work involved in examining letters, applications and complaints from the working people in the Party's central bodies, the correctness of the execution of the Party budget, including the payment, collection and accounting of Party dues, and also the financial and economic activities of the enterprises and institutions of the CPSU Central Committee.

37. The CC CPSU shall hold not less than one plenary meeting every six months. Alternate members of the Central Committee shall have a consultative voice at sessions of the CC plenary meetings.

38. The Central Committee of the Communist Party of the Soviet

Union elects a Politbureau to direct the work of the Party between plenary meetings of the CC, and a Secretariat to direct current work, chiefly the selection of cadres and the verification of the fulfilment of Party decisions. The Central Committee elects the General Secretary of the CC CPSU.

39. The Central Committee of the Communist Party of the Soviet Union organizes the Party Control Committee of the CC.

The Party Control Committee of the CC CPSU:

(a) verifies the observance of Party discipline by members and candidate members of the CPSU, and takes action against Communists who violate the Programme and the Rules of the Party and Party or state discipline, and against violators of Party ethics;

(b) considers appeals against decisions of Central Committees of the Communist Parties of the Union Republics or of territorial and regional Party committees on expelling members from the Party or imposing penalties upon them.

40. In the interim between Party congresses the CPSU Central Committee may convene, should the need arise, an All-Union Party Conference to discuss pressing Party policy issues. The procedure of holding an All-Union Party Conference is determined by the CC CPSU.

V. Republican, Territorial, Regional, Area, City and District Party Organizations

41. The republican, territorial, regional, area, city and district Party organizations and their committees are guided in their activities by the Programme and the Rules of the CPSU, carry out all work for the implementation of Party policy and organize the fulfilment of the directives of the CPSU Central Committee within the Republics, territories, regions, areas, cities and districts concerned.

42. The basic duties of republican, territorial, regional, area, city and district Party organizations, and of their leading bodies, are:

(a) political and organizational work among the masses, mobilization of Communists, of all working people for carrying out the tasks of communist construction, accelerating socio-economic development on the basis of scientific and technological progress, increasing the efficiency of social production, raising labour productivity and improving product quality, fulfilling state plans and socialist commitments, and ensuring the steady rise in the material and cultural standards of the working people;

(b) organization of ideological work, propaganda of Marxism-Leninism, promotion of the communist awareness of the working people, guidance of the local press, radio and television, and control over the activities of scientific, cultural and educational institutions;

(c) guidance of Soviets of People's Deputies, trade unions, the YCL, the cooperative and other public organizations through the Communists working in them, and the increasingly broader involvement of working people in the activities of these organizations, development of the initiative and activity of the masses as an essential condition for the further in-depth development of socialist democracy;

(d) strict observance of the Leninist principles and methods of leadership, the affirmation of the Leninist style in Party work, in all spheres of state and economic management, securing the unity of ideological, organizational and economic activities, the strengthening of socialist law, of state and labour discipline, order and organization in all sectors;

(e) implementation of the personnel policy, education of personnel in the spirit of communist ideology, fostering moral integrity and a high sense of responsibility to the Party and the people for the work entrusted to them;

(f) organization of various Party institutions and enterprises within the bounds of their Republic, territory, region, area, city or district and guidance of their activities; distribution of Party funds within the given organization; regular reports to the higher Party body and accountability to it for their work.

Leading Bodies of Republican, Territorial and Regional Party Organizations

43. The highest body of republican, territorial and regional Party organizations is the congress of the Communist Party of a Union Republic, the territorial or regional Party conference and, in the interim, the Central Committee of the Communist Party of a Union Republic, and the territorial or regional committee.

44. A regular congress of the Communist Party of a Union Republic shall be convened by the Central Committee of the Communist Party not less than once in five years. A regular territorial or regional Party conference shall be convened by the territorial or regional committee once every two–three years. Extraordinary (emergency) congresses and conferences are convened by the decision of the Central Committee of the Communist Party of a Union Republic, the territorial or regional committee, or on the demand of one-third of the total membership of the organizations belonging to the republican, territorial or regional Party organization.

The rates of representation at congresses of the Communist Parties of the Union Republics, at territorial and regional conferences are established by the respective Party committees.

A congress of the Communist Party of a Union Republic or a territorial or regional conference hears the report of the Central Committee of the Communist Party of the Union Republic or of the territorial or regional committee, and the report of the auditing commission, discusses at its own discretion other matters of Party, economic and cultural development, and elects the Central Committee of the Communist Party of the Union Republic or the territorial or regional committee, the auditing commission and delegates to the Congress of the CPSU.

In the interim between congresses of the Communist Parties of the Union Republics, the Central Committees of the Communist Parties may convene, whenever necessary, republican Party conferences to discuss topical questions concerning Party organizations' activities. The procedure for holding republican Party conferences is determined by the Central Committees of the Communist Parties of the Union Republics.

45. The Central Committees of the Communist Parties of the Union Republics, the territorial and regional committees elect bureaus, including secretaries of the committees. The secretaries must have a Party standing of not less than five years. The plenary meetings of the committees approve the heads of departments of these committees, chairmen of Party control commissions and editors of Party newspapers and journals.

The Central Committees of the Communist Parties of the Union Republics, territorial and regional Party committees set up secretariats to attend to current affairs and verify the implementation of decisions.

46. Plenary meetings of the Central Committees of the Communist Parties of the Union Republics, of territorial and regional committees shall be convened at least once every four months.

47. The Central Committees of the Communist Parties of the Union Republics, the territorial and regional committees direct the area, city and district Party organizations, inspect their work and regularly hear reports of the respective Party committees.

Party organizations in Autonomous Republics, and in autonomous and other regions forming part of a Union Republic or a territory, function under the guidance of the Central Committees of the Communist Parties of the Union Republics or respective territorial committees.

Leading Bodies of Area, City and District (Rural and Urban) Party Organizations

48. The highest body of an area, city or district Party organization is the area, city or district Party conference or the general meeting of communists convened by the area, city or district committee once in 2–3 years, as well as an extraordinary conference or general meeting convened by the decision of the respective committee or on the demand of one-third of the total membership of the Party organization concerned.

The area, city or district conference (meeting) hears reports of the committee and the auditing commission, discusses at its own discretion other questions of Party, economic and cultural development, and elects the area, city or district committee, the auditing commission and delegates to the regional or territorial conference or the congress of the Communist Party of the Union Republic.

The rates of representation at the area, city and district conferences are established by the respective Party committee.

49. The area, city or district committee elects a bureau, including the committee secretaries, and approves heads of committee departments, the chairman of the Party commission and newspaper editors. The secretaries of the area, city and district committees must have a Party standing of at least five years. The committee secretaries are approved by the respective regional or territorial committee, or the Central Committee of the Communist Party of the Union Republic.

50. The area, city or district committee sets up the primary Party organizations, directs their work, regularly hears reports on the work of Party organizations, and keeps a register of Communists.

51. The plenary meeting of the area, city or district committee is convened at least once every three months.

VI. Primary Party Organizations

52. The primary Party organizations are the basis of the Party.

Primary Party organizations are formed at the places of work of Party members – factories, state farms and other enterprises, collective farms, units of the Armed Forces, offices, educational establishments, etc., wherever there are not less than three Party members. If necessary, primary Party organizations may also be formed on the residential principle.

In individual cases, with the approval of the regional or territorial committee, or of the Central Committee of the Communist Party of the Union Republic, Party organizations may be formed within the framework of several enterprises that make up a production association and are located, as a rule, on the territory of one or several districts in the same city.

53. At enterprises, collective farms and institutions with over 50 members and candidate members of the CPSU, shop, sectional, farm, team, departmental, and other such Party organizations may be formed within one primary Party organization with the approval of the district, city or area committee.

Within shop, sectional, etc., organizations, and also within primary Party organizations with less than 50 members and candidate members, Party groups may be formed in the teams and other production units.

54. The highest body of the primary Party organization is the Party meeting, which is convened at least once a month. In Party organizations with shop organizations, both general and shop meetings are held at least once every two months.

In large Party organizations with a membership of more than 300 Communists, a general Party meeting is convened when necessary as scheduled by the Party committee or on the demand of several shop Party organizations.

55. To attend to current affairs, the primary or shop Party organization elects a bureau for a term of two or three years. The number of its members is fixed by the Party meeting. Primary and shop Party organizations with less than 15 Party members do not elect a bureau. Instead, they elect a secretary and a deputy secretary of the Party organization. Elections in these organizations are held every year.

Secretaries of primary and shop Party organizations must have a Party standing of at least one year.

Primary Party organizations with less than 150 Party members shall have, as a rule, no salaried functionaries relieved from their regular work.

56. At large enterprises and institutions with more than 300 Party members and candidate members, and if necessary at organizations with over 100 Communists, by virtue of specific production conditions and territorial dispersion, and subject to the approval of the regional committee, territorial committee or the Central Committee of the Communist Party of the Union Republic, Party committees may be formed, with shop Party organizations granted the rights of primary Party organizations.

The Party organizations of collective farms, state farms and other agricultural enterprises may form Party committees if there are no less than 50 Communists in them.

In individual cases, given the approval of the regional or territorial Party committee, or the Central Committee of the Communist Party of the Union Republic, Party organizations numbering more than 500 Communists may form Party committees in the larger shops, and the Party organizations in production sectors may be granted the rights of a primary Party organization.

The Party committees are elected for a term of 2–3 years. Their numerical composition is fixed by the general Party meeting or conference.

Party committees, Party bureaus and secretaries of primary and shop Party organizations regularly inform Communists of their work at Party meetings.

57. The Party committees of primary Party organizations with more than 1,000 Communists may be granted, with the approval of the Central Committee of the Communist Party of the Union Republic, the rights of a district Party committee in matters of admission to the CPSU, of keeping a register of members and candidate members of the Party and of considering the personal cases of Communists.

These organizations may elect enlarged Party committees within which bureaus are formed to guide day-to-day work.

58. In its activities the primary Party organization is guided by the Programme and the Rules of the CPSU. It is the political nucleus of a work collective, it conducts its activities in the midst of the working people, rallies them round the Party, organizes them to fulfil the tasks of communist construction, takes an active part in implementing the Party's personnel policy.

The primary Party organization:

(a) admits new members to the CPSU;

(b) educates Communists in the spirit of loyalty to the Party cause, ideological staunchness and communist ethics;

(c) organizes the study by Communists of Marxist-Leninist theory in close connection with the practice of communist construction and combats any manifestations of bourgeois ideology, revisionism and dogmatism, backward views and moods;

(d) ensures the growing vanguard role of Communists in work and in socio-political life, their exemplary behaviour in everyday life, hears reports of CPSU members and candidate members on the fulfilment of their statutory duties and Party assignments;

(e) acts as the organizer of the working people in carrying out the tasks of economic and social development, heads the socialist emulation movement for the fulfilment of state plans and commitments, the intensification of production, the raising of labour productivity and product quality, the extensive introduction of the achievements of science and technology and advanced experience into production, mobilizes the working people for tapping internal reserves, works for the rational, economical use of material, labour and financial resources, shows concern for the protection and growth of public wealth, for the improvement of people's working and living conditions;

(f) conducts political education and propaganda work, educates the working people in the spirit of devotion to the ideas of communism, Soviet patriotism and friendship among peoples, helps them achieve a high level of political culture, enhances their social activism and sense of responsibility;

(g) helps Communists, all working people get used to participation in socialist self-government, ensures the growing role of the work collective in managing the affairs of enterprises and organizations, guides the activities of the trade union, YCL and other public organizations;

(h) on the basis of extensive criticism and self-criticism, combats cases of bureaucracy, parochialism, departmentalism, violations of state, labour and production discipline, thwarts attempts to deceive the state, acts against negligence, waste and extravagance, works to affirm a temperate way of life.

59. The primary Party organizations at enterprises in industry, transport, communications, construction, material and technical supply, trade, public catering, communal and public welfare services, at collective and state farms and other agricultural enterprises, design organizations and drafting offices, research institutes, educational establishments, cultural and medical institutions, enjoy the right to control the work of the administration.

The Party organizations at ministries, state committees, and other central and local government and economic bodies and departments exercise control over the fulfilment of Party and government directives and the observance of Soviet laws by the apparatus. They must actively contribute to the improvement of the work of the apparatus, the selection, placement and education of its staff, enhance their responsibility for the matter in hand, for the development of a particular sector and of public services, take measures to strengthen state discipline, resolutely combat bureaucracy and red tape, inform the appropriate Party bodies in good time of shortcomings in the work of the respective offices and individuals, regardless of the post the latter may hold.[3]

3. Primary Party organizations may set up commissions to exercise the right of control over the administration's activities, and the work of the apparatus in certain production spheres.

VII. The Party and the State and Public Organizations

60. The CPSU, acting within the framework of the USSR Constitution, exercises political leadership of state and public organizations, directs and coordinates their activities.

The Party organizations, Communists working in state and public organizations see to it that these organizations fully exercise their constitutional powers and statutory rights and duties, and that they extensively involve working people in management and in deciding political, economic and social questions.

Party organizations do not supplant government, trade union, cooperative and other public organizations, and do not allow the functions of the Party and other bodies to be mixed.

61. Party groups are formed at congresses, conferences and meetings convened by state and public organizations, as well as in the elected bodies of these organizations with at least three Party members. The task of these groups is to carry out Party policy in the respective non-Party organizations, to enhance Communists' influence on the state of affairs in these organizations, to develop the democratic principles in their activities, to strengthen Party and state discipline, to combat bureaucracy, to verify the fulfilment of Party and government directives.

62. The work of Party groups within non-Party organizations is guided by the respective Party body: the CPSU Central Committee, the Central Committee of the Communist Party of the Union Republic, territorial, regional, area, city or district Party committee.

VIII. The Party and the YCL

63. The All-Union Leninist Young Communist League is an independent public and political organization of young people, an active assistant and reserve of the Party. The YCL helps the Party educate the youth in the communist spirit, draw it into the practice of building the new society and running state and public affairs, and raise a generation of harmoniously developed people prepared to work and to defend their Soviet Motherland.

64. The YCL organizations must actively promote Party directives in all spheres of production and social life. They enjoy the right of broad initiative in discussing and raising in the appropriate Party organizations questions related to the work of enterprises, collective farms, institutions or educational establishments, and directly take part in solving them, especially if they pertain to the work, everyday life, training and education of young people.

65. The YCL works under the guidance of the Communist Party

of the Soviet Union. The work of the local YCL organizations is guided and monitored by the appropriate republican, territorial, regional, area, city and district Party organizations.

In carrying out the communist education of young people, in mobilizing them for the fulfilment of concrete production and social tasks, local Party bodies and primary Party organizations rely on the YCL organizations, support their useful initiatives, give them every assistance in their activities.

66. Members of the YCL who have been admitted to the CPSU cease to belong to the YCL the moment they join the Party, provided they are not members of elected YCL bodies and do not work as YCL functionaries.

IX. Party Organizations in the Armed Forces

67. Party organizations in the Armed Forces are guided in their work by the Programme and the Rules of the CPSU and operate on the basis of instructions issued by the Central Committee. They ensure the implementation of the Party's policy in the Armed Forces, rally servicemen round the Communist Party, educate them in the spirit of Marxism-Leninism and boundless loyalty to the socialist Motherland, actively further the unity of the army and the people, concern themselves with enhancing troops' combat preparedness and with strengthening army discipline, mobilize servicemen for carrying out the tasks of combat and political training, for becoming skilled in the use of new hardware and weapons and for irreproachably fulfilling their military duty and the orders and instructions of the command.

68. Party work in the Armed Forces is guided by the CPSU Central Committee through political bodies. The Chief Political Administration of the Soviet Army and Navy functions as a department of the CC CPSU.

The chiefs of the political administrations of military districts and fleets, and the chiefs of the political departments of armies, flotillas and formations must have a Party standing of five years.

69. The Party organizations and political bodies of the Armed Forces maintain close contacts with local Party committees, and regularly brief them on the political work carried out in the military units. The secretaries of army Party organizations and chiefs of political bodies participate in the work of local Party committees.

X. Party Funds

70. The funds of the Party and its organizations are derived from

membership dues, incomes from Party enterprises and other revenue.

The CPSU Central Committee decides how Party funds are to be used.

71. The monthly membership dues for Party members and candidate members are as follows:

Monthly earnings	*Dues*	
up to 70 roubles	10 kopeks	
71 to 100 roubles	20 kopeks	
101 to 150 roubles	1.0 per cent	
151 to 200 roubles	1.5 per cent	of the
201 to 250 roubles	2.0 per cent	monthly
251 to 300 roubles	2.5 per cent	earnings
over 300 roubles	3.0 per cent	

72. Candidate members pay admission dues of two per cent of their monthly earnings.

Index

For Product Safety Concerns and Information please contact our EU
representative GPSR@taylorandfrancis.com
Taylor & Francis Verlag GmbH, Kaufingerstraße 24, 80331 München, Germany

www.ingramcontent.com/pod-product-compliance
Lightning Source LLC
Chambersburg PA
CBHW050522280326
41932CB00014B/2418